SOUTHERN OREGON CROSS COUNTRY SKI TRAILS

by JOHN W. LUND

Printed By
Smith-Bates Printing
Klamath Falls, Oregon

Published by John W. Lund
P.O. Box 2126
Oretech Branch
Klamath Falls, OR 97601

Photos and maps by the author
Edited by Joan M. Foster
Pen and ink sketches by B.L. Syler

Cover photograph: Crater Lake

ISBN O-9619389-1-9

TABLE OF CONTENTS

LOCATION MAP   4

INTRODUCTION   7

AREA A: LEMOLO LAKE   16

          A1.   Pipeline   18
          A2.   Basket   18
          A3.   Lemolo Run   18
          A4.   Sidewinder   19
          A5.   Big Buck   19
          A6.   Elk Flat   19
          A7.   Bobtail   20
          A8.   Poole Creek   20

AREA B: DIAMOND LAKE   22

          B1.   Cinnamon Butte & Wits End   24
          B2.   The Pizza Connection   27
          B3.   North Diamond   29
          B4.   North Crater   31
          B5.   Howlock   35
          B6.   Thielsen   38
          B7.   Spruce Ridge   40
          B8.   Horse 'N Teal   42
          B9.   Silent Creek   44
          B10. Mt. Bailey   46
          B11. Summit Rock   49
          B12. Pacific Crest Trail   51
          B13. Diamond Lake Snowmobile Trails   56
                a.   Lake West   56
                b.   Diamond Lake Loop   56
                c.   Crater Lake - North Rim   57

AREA C: CHEMULT   58

AREA D: CRATER LAKE NATIONAL PARK   60

          D1.   Hemlock   62
          D2.   Raven   64
          D3.   Wizard Island   65
          D4.   Sun Notch   67
          D5.   Dutton Creek   70
          D6.   Lightening Springs   73
          D7.   Grayback   76
          D8.   Crater Peak   78
          D9.   Crater Lake Rim   80
          D10. Union Creek   85

D11. Stuart Falls   88

AREA E: UNION CREEK   91

         E1. Union Creek   93
         E2. Thousand Springs   96
         E3. Rocktop   99
         E4. Huckleberry   101
         E5. Pipeline   103
         E6. Wagon Camp   105
         E7. Lake West   107
         E8. Hamaker Loop   111

AREA F: SKY LAKES WILDERNESS   114

         F1. Seven Lakes Basin   116
         F2. Cherry Creek   120
         F3. Pacific Crest   122
         F4. Squaw Lake   126
         F5. Pelican Butte   128

AREA G: FREMONT - LAKEVIEW   130

         G1. Gearhart Mountain Wilderness   131
         G2. Ewauna Loop   134
         G3. Pass Loop   136
         G4. Grade Loop   138
         G5. Warner Canyon   140
         G6. Bull Prairie   140
         G7. Horse Prairie   140

AREA H: FISH LAKE - LAKE OF THE WOODS   142

         H1. Sunset   144
         H2. Lake of the Woods   146
         H3. Billie Creek Loop   148
         H4. Lower Canal   151
         H5. Upper Canal   154
         H6. Fourmile Lake   156
         H7. Powerline   158
         H8. Fish Lake Tie   160
         H9. South Rye   162
         H10. Lund's Link   165
         H11. Lollipop   167
         H12. Jellybean   170
         H13. Peppermint   171
         H14. Candy "Cain"   171
         H15. Brown Mountain   172

AREA I: KLAMATH WEST   173

          I1. Hamaker and Chase Mountain - Bear Valley 174
               Mt. Lakes Wilderness   177
          I2. Varney Creek   179
          I3. Clover Creek   181
          I4. Mountain Lakes   183
          I5. Mountain Lakes Loop   185

AREA J: BUCK PRAIRIE   187

          J1. Buck Prairie Loop   189
          J2. Cottonwood Glades   192
          J3. Table Mountain Loop   194
          J4. Campers Cove   198

AREA K: MT. ASHLAND   201

          K1. Siskiyou Summit Road   203
          K2. Bull Gap   207
          K3. Pacific Crest Loop   211

APPENDIX I: HISTORY OF SOUTHERN OREGON
              CROSS COUNTRY SKI RACES   213

APPENDIX II: RESORT ADDRESSES, SKI CLUB ADDRESSES,
              AND FEDERAL AGENCY ADDRESSES   220

4000 year old cave drawing found in northern Scandinavia.

3

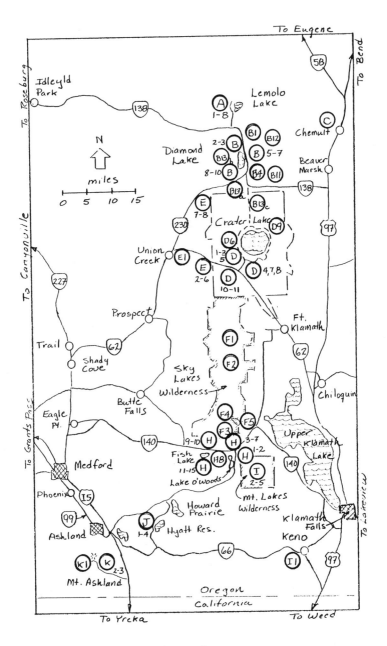

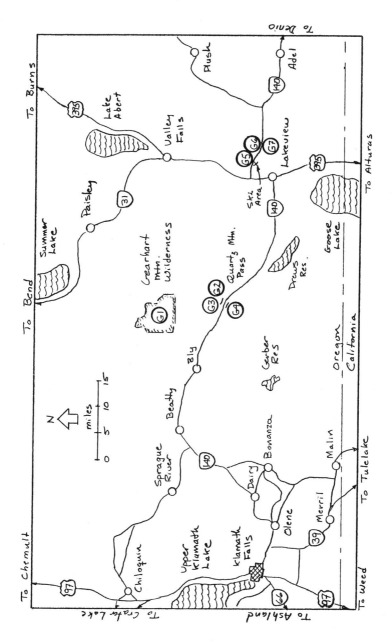

......
Two roads diverged in a wood, and I -
I took the one less traveled by,
And that has made all the difference.

- Robert Frost

INTRODUCTION

Outside of Crater Lake National Park, cross country skiing in Southern Oregon has received little notice. However, in the last 20 years, I have skied over 300 miles on scenic trails - many of which are little used. So, come and enjoy the scenery, the sunshine and the solitude.

Southern Oregon is dominated by prominent volcanic peaks and dotted with many lakes. Most trails offer a variety of terrain and views as well as ample sunshine. Another advantage of skiing in this area is the many lodges available for refreshment and relaxation. Most of the trails start or end near one of the ten ski areas or resort complexes. Some have overnight lodging and rent skis. See the Appendix for a list of lodges and ski areas.

The trails cross five National Forests (Umpqua, Rogue River, Winema, Fremont and Klamath), Bureau of Land Management land (Medford District), and Crater Lake National Park. In many cases, maps of the ski and snowmobile trails are available at their offices or the trailhead. See the Appendix for a list of offices.

Trail Selection

I selected approximately 80 trails in a region shaped like an inverted "T", starting with Lemolo Lake in the north to the Lake of the Woods area in the south, and from Lakeview in the east to Mt. Ashland in the west. The location and number of these trails are shown on the overview map after the Table of Contents. I have identified each area with a letter, and individual trails by number; thus the Spruce Ridge Trail near Diamond Lake (area B) is designated trail B7. These are the most popular trails in the region; however, with abundant public land and many logging roads, there are many potential trails the adventurous skier can explore and use. These trails usually have little or no snowmobile traffic.

7

Trail Description

Each trail description includes a difficulty rating, starting point, length in miles and kilometers, elevation change and a list of the appropriate maps. Each of these headings is explained below.

My trail ratings - beginning, intermediate and advanced - are similar to the federal agencies' Easiest, More Difficult, Most Difficult. They are based on average snow conditions and may change if you are traveling up or downhill, in icy or wet snow, or if you must break trail.

BEGINNING: A trail with little elevation change and less than a five-mile (8-km) round-trip. These trails are very popular, are usually well marked, and a track is broken. They can be negotiated by the novice skier.

INTERMEDIATE: A trail with moderate elevation change requiring snowplowing downhill to check descent and herringboning to climb uphill. The round-trip length is usually under ten miles (16 km). It is marked, but a trail is not necessarily broken. Normally, a skier using this trail has at least one season's experience and is in reasonable physical condition.

ADVANCED: A trail for the skier with several years of experience. The trail will have many steep and narrow sections requiring advanced techniques. Often, the trail is unmarked, unbroken and exposed to wind, avalanche, or whiteout. The trail will have extensive elevation gain or loss and cover a long distance. Skiers should carry winter survival equipment, map and compass.

Parking areas or other trails are identified as the best starting points. The elevation is an indication of potential snow conditions. In Southern Oregon, little skiing is available below 3000 feet; from 3000 to 4000 feet the skiing is marginal and will last for no more than one month (usually during December and January); elevation between 4000 and 5000 feet is usually the minimum for adequate snow lasting for up to three months (December through February); elevation above 5000 feet provides the best chance for good skiing from mid-November through mid-March. Areas such as Crater Lake rim (7000 feet) may have a ski season from October through May. The varied snow conditions at lower elevations make waxing a problem. In March and April, I have skied on everything from wet snow, to pine needles and snow, tree limbs and bare ground.

The trail length is given to the nearest 0.1 mile and in kilometers (1.0 mile = 1.6 km). Note that 0.1 mile is approximately 500 feet or 150 meters (slightly more than the length of one-and-one-half football fields). The distances are determined by at least two different methods: measurements from maps, trail signs, estimates from skiing or hiking times, or from automobile odometer readings. These distances and those in the detailed descriptions are accurate within 10%. The detailed description of each trail will assist you in locating key landmarks and avoiding wrong turns. What looks obvious in the summer is often buried or masked in the winter.

Skiing time will vary widely depending upon your ability, snow conditions, trail markings, whether there is a broken track, and if you are skiing uphill or downhill. These are rough rules of thumb:

1 - 2 mph (2 - 3 km/hr):   beginning skier; wet snow;
                           breaking trail; climbing uphill

2 - 4 mph (3 - 6 km/hr):   intermediate skier; average snow
                           conditions; level skiing

4 - 6 mph (6 - 10 km/hr): advanced skier; broken track;
                           dry snow; downhill skiing

6 - 11 mph (10 - 18 km/hr): winners in citizen cross
                           country ski races

11 - 13 mph (18 - 21 km/hr): winners in professional and
                           Olympic ski races

The elevation change is given to the high or low point on the trails, with some intermediate points noted. This is some indication of difficulty. The easiest trails gain elevation going in, making the return trip easier and quicker. Be sure you can negotiate the faster downhill trail.

Both Geological Survey (USGS) and Forest Service/Bureau of Land Management (USFS/BLM) maps are listed. Most of the USGS maps are 15 minute quadrangle sheets issued in the 1950's and 1960's; thus many of the road and trail locations have changed. Fortunately, a new series of 7.5 minute quadrangle sheets are being issued for areas in Southern Oregon. For example, a set of preliminary sheets is available for Crater Lake National Park; however to replace the old map, it takes four of these large sheets to cover only the rim road and four more for the rest of the park.

Sketch Maps

A sketch map shows the key terrain features for each trail.
All trails are labelled with capital letters, and the one
described is marked with a heavier symbol. Parking and major
highways are shown. From the start, each mile of the trail is
marked. The following map symbols are used:

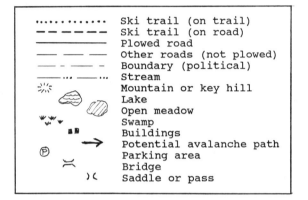

••••••••••••	Ski trail (on trail)
— — — — —	Ski trail (on road)
———————	Plowed road
—— —— ——	Other roads (not plowed)
—— - —— -	Boundary (political)
———••• ——•••	Stream
✵	Mountain or key hill
(lake shape)	Lake
(meadow shape)	Open meadow
ᵥ ᵥ ᵥ	Swamp
▪▫	Buildings
→	Potential avalanche path
Ⓟ	Parking area
⏝⏜	Bridge
)(	Saddle or pass

Trail Signing

The standard cross country ski trail marking on federal lands
is a blue diamond attached to trees 8 to 15 feet from the
ground. These may be supplemented with blue trailhead signs
giving the trail name and distances to key points. Some of the
diamonds have a black arrow indicating a change in direction
(sometimes indicated by leaning the top of the diamond to the
left or right). Snowmobile trails are marked with orange
diamonds, and also use a black arrow for direction changes. Ski
trails that follow summer hiking trails may have wooden, engraved
signs and single or double blazes on trees (these may be buried
by the snow). There are many exceptions to these standards, such
as a silver-gray diamond on parts of the Pacific Crest Trail,
orange diamonds on some BLM trails, a small metal rectangle with
one orange and one red side attached to trees in Crater Lake
National Park, or diamonds with dark blue, black or white
centers. Recently the Forest Service began removing all markings
on wilderness trails such as the Pacific Crest Trail, since
regional policy prohibits marking these trails except at
trailheads and trail junctions. I indicate the type of markings
on each trail; however the responsible agency may change these

without notice.

Many of the trails in Southern Oregon are maintained and marked in cooperation with local cross country ski organizations, resort owners and ski rental concessionaires. Special recognition should go to the Grants Pass Nordic Club and the Diamond Lake Nordic Center for their leadership and hard work.

Forest Service Road Signing

The National Forest roads in Region 6 (Oregon and Washington) have been renumbered for consistency from forest to forest and to provide more information. The detailed trail descriptions use these numbers.

ARTERIAL ROADS: These primary roads connect to state and country roads. They are generally through routes with access to and through large areas of land. They are assigned a two digit road number, e.g., Road 43.

COLLECTOR ROADS: These secondary roads serve medium-sized areas of land. They connect to the arterial routes and may or may not be through routes. They are assigned a four digit road number, e.g., Road 4357. The first two digits indicate the arterial route providing access to the collector road, in this case, arterial Road 43.

LOCAL ROADS: These are usually low standard administrative access roads (I refer to them as spurs). They are generally dead end, providing access to a small area of land. These most often connect to a collector road and are assigned a seven digit number, e.g., Road 4357-060. Normally only the last three digits are shown on maps and displayed on vertical fiberglass markers at the shoulder of the road. These latter markers are often covered by snow. Each forest has its own system for assigning the three digits to the local road; however numbers generally increase as you proceed down a collector road. The last digit, other than zero, indicates a spur off the local road.

Parking

Parking is limited at most trailheads, so I recommend car-pooling. I have indicated the location and the approximate spaces available in the detailed description. Many of these parking areas require a Sno-Park permit. These permits, costing less than $10, provide monies to the State Highway Fund for plowing roads and parking areas in winter recreation areas. They are available at all Motor Vehicles Division field offices, many resorts, ski shops and sporting goods stores. The permit must be displayed on the dash or front window of your vehicle.

Hazards

Four major hazards can confront the cross country skier: storms, avalanches, hypothermia and getting lost. Check the local weather reports and call nearby resorts for information about storms. Be alert to the signs of potential avalanches, but my sketch maps show the locations of the most serious dangers. Generally the worst avalanche locations in Southern Oregon are on portions of the rim drive of Crater Lake National Park, on the slopes of Mt. Thielsen and Mt. Bailey near Diamond Lake, and along the north (lee) side of the ridge of the Siskiyou Summit Road behind Mt. Ashland. If you are skiing in an avalanche area, carry a shovel and probes or poles.

You should recognize the symptoms of hypothermia and be able to treat it. Hypothermia occurs in weather above or below freezing; most hypothermia cases develop in air temperatures between 30 and 50 degrees F. Wind and rain or wet snow are the main culprits; thus protection against these elements is essential. Finally, to minimize the chances of becoming lost, carry map and compass and look back over your shoulder as you ski in, so that you can recognize the trail on the way back. Always carry emergency repair equipment, survival gear, and most important, and know your limitations. It is better to turn back and not achieve your goal than to have someone come looking for you. An excellent brochure, "Winter Recreation Safety Guide," is available from most Forest Service offices.

Trail Ethics

Skiing on public land (and on private land with permission) is a privilege seldom available in the Midwest and East, but requires you to accept certain responsibilities. A "Winter Recreation Code of Ethics" has been endorsed by the Southern Oregon High Lakes Group, an organization of local snowmobile, cross country ski groups and government agencies. I feel that these principles are important enough to reprint for you.

1. I will be a good sportsman (-woman). I recognize that people judge all winter recreationists by individual actions. I will give assistance to those in distress.

2. I will plan my outing according to my ability, endurance, equipment, and will check current weather reports. I will tell someone where I am going and when I expect to return.

3. I will keep to the right when meeting another winter recreationist. I will yield the right-of-way to traffic moving downhill.

4. I will slow down and use caution when approaching or overtaking another.

5. When stopping, I will not block the trail.

6. I will learn to recognize winter trail signs, blazes and maps. I will respect and obey designated trails, closed areas and private property.

7. I will park considerately, taking no more space than needed, without blocking other vehicles and without impeding access to trails. I will carpool where possible to conserve parking spaces.

8. I will pack my litter home.

9. I will not harass wildlife.

10. I will leave my pets at home.

I want to especially emphasize the last point. Please do not bring dogs on the trails - they are a hazard to other skiers, break up the trail, and leave messes behind (we don't need that kind of ski wax). If you must bring your dog, ski away from the marked ski trails.

Ski Organizations and Races

Three cross country ski clubs in Southern Oregon have organized trips, work on trails and sponsor citizen ski races - the Alla Mage Skiers of Klamath Falls, the Southern Oregon branch of the Oregon Nordic Club in Medford/Ashland, and the Grants Pass Nordic Club. A fourth organization, the Fremont Highlanders Ski Club, Inc. in Lakeview, is taking an interest in developing cross country skiing trails. All have newsletters and meetings - their addresses are provided in the Appendix.

Three major ski races are sponsored by these groups: The Crater Lake Wilderness Races in early February (Alla Mage/Crater Lake National Park); Lake of the Woods/Fish Lake Citizen Race in late February (Grants Pass Nordic Club); and the John Day Memorial Race in late February (Oregon Nordic Club/Diamond Lake Nordic Center). All are citizen races, with several distances and age classes. Contact the individual ski club for details. The histories of two of these races are so interesting that I have included them in the Appendix.

Acknowledgements

Many Federal employees have provided trail information and maps, as well as reviewing my descriptions, but are not responsible for my opinions or errors. Specifically, I would like to thank: Craig Miller, Gordon Chadband, Dick Cleveland, and Jim Galaba of the Winema NF; Ken Rogers, Cliff Curtis, Robert Brackett, and Bill Selby of the Fremont NF; Rick Ley of the Rogue River NF; Tom Spencer of the Umpqua NF; Hank Tanski and Fred Vanhorn of Crater Lake National Park; and Fred Thomlin of the BLM. A special thanks to Margaret Holman of the Ashland Ranger District of the Rogue River National Forest for discussing many of the details of this book and spending time with me in the field.

I have many friends who have helped me in some way over the last 20 years. These include students from my many cross country ski classes at Oregon Institute of Technology (OIT), the student leaders in the Outdoor Program at OIT, the Alla Mage and Nordic Ski Clubs, and the following people: Jim, Walt, Ed, Judy, Shelly, Louis, Don and Carol, Sue, Richard, Helen, Dan, Mike, Gary, Sherm, and Joan. J. D. Lewis assisted and gave advice on my photographs, B. L. Syler provided the sketches at the bottom of the pages, and Taylor Cain provided background and information on trails in the Union Creek area.

Joan M. Foster has spent many hours editing my manuscripts and offering critical comments. She has improved my "engineering" approach to writing in many ways. I very much appreciate her time, effort and friendship. I would also like to thank my son Dave for helping me with many of the ski classes. Finally, I would like to thank my parents for their patience and encouragement.

A. LEMOLO LAKE

Lemolo Lake is located 12 miles north of Diamond Lake, just off Highway 138 on Forest Service Road 2610. It is about 75 miles to Roseburg along the North Umpqua River. The lake lies in a small basin at elevation 4142'.

Th Lemolo Lake Resort, in cooperation with the Umpqua National Forest, has developed about 10 miles of groomed beginning trails to the west of the lake and resort. It is an excellent place for a family outing. The trails are well marked with blue diamonds and junction signs, and have interesting names such as Bobtail, Basket and Sidewinder. The resort is open all year, providing lodging, restaurant, grocery and gas services. If you are lucky, in the spring you might see an elk - I saw numerous tracks in early April.

The trails usually follow dirt and gravel roads, but numerous interesting paths, such as Sidewinder, are a challenge. For the more advanced skier, Basket Butte (5250') and Elephant Mountain (a ridge varying between 5600' and 5900' in elevation) provide some steep runs. Since the trails are all between 4100' and 4400' elevation, snow does not remain on the ground as long as it does in the High Cascades - check with the resort for snow conditions (address and phone number given in the Appendix).

LEMOLO LAKE TRAILS - GENERAL

The trails are all interconnected, thus you have a variety of routes to choose - some in the trees and some in the open. I would suggest starting up Pipeline or Lemolo Run and then skiing downhill through any of the connecting trails back to the resort.

Trail Difficulty:	Beginning on roads
Starting Point:	Lemolo Lake Resort; elevation 4190'
Trail Length:	1 to 5 miles (1.6 to 8.0 km) round trip
Elevation Change:	210' maximum gain from the resort
Maps:	USGS: Summit Lake (15 min.) USFS: Umpqua National Forest; Diamond and Lemolo Lake Nordic Trails - Umpqua National Forest

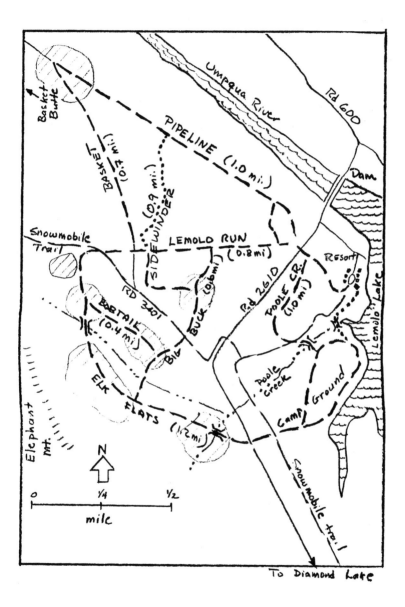

Basket Butte

Umpqua River

Rd 600

PIPELINE (1.0 mi.)

BASKET (0.7 mi.)

Dam

SIDEWINDER (0.9 mi.)

Snowmobile Trail

LEMOLO RUN (0.8mi)

Resort

RD 3401

BUCK (0.6mi)

Rd 2610

POOLE CR. (1.0 mi)

Lemolo Lake

BOBTAIL (0.4 mi)

BIG ELK FLATS (1.2mi)

Poole Creek

Camp Ground

Elephant Mt.

N

0   ¼   ½
mile

Snowmobile trail

To Diamond Lake

A1. PIPELINE

All trails start from the west end of the resort parking lot turnaround, just past the gas station. Ski a little over 0.2 miles north west, past the turnoff on the left to Poole Creek Trail and cross the main highway. On the other side turn right to start Pipeline Trail. The trail to the left is the start of Lemolo Run.

Pipeline, named after the water pipeline to the power plant in the canyon below, is a 1.0-mile (1.6-km) long trail. It initially is level and at 0.2 miles passes a connecting trail to Lemolo Run. At 0.4 mile, a road turns off to the right - ski straight ahead and uphill - this is the longest hill of the trail system. At 0.6 mile, pass the turnoff to the Sidewinder Trail on the left. The trail levels off in a clearing near the top where it intersects Basket Trail.

You are now at elevation 4400', the highest point on the trail system. Basket Butte is almost due west, and the road continues around behind the butte (not part of the trail system). Turn sharp left to ski down Basket Trail.

A2. BASKET

Basket trail is 0.7 miles (1.1 km) long, downhill from the intersection with Pipeline, mainly through an open area. At the bottom it intersects Lemolo Run as indicated by a sign. If you continue ahead, this road leads back to the main highway; however, in 0.2 mile it becomes a snowmobile road.

Turning left takes you down Lemolo Run. Turning right, which is poorly marked, takes you over to Elk Flats trail about 0.2 mile away.

A3. LEMOLO RUN

Lemolo Run is a straight trail like Pipeline. It starts at the junction with Pipeline on the west side of the main highway near the resort. At 0.1 mile, the short connection to Pipeline comes in on the right. You are now in fairly dense timber and climbing slightly; at 0.3 mile Big Buck Trail drops down to the left. Sidewinder crosses at 0.5 mile, and at 0.6 mile the trail ties into the lower end of Basket. Continuing on across Basket (the trail is poorly marked) through the woods, down a bank and across a snowmobile trail, this trail ends at 0.8 mile and connects with the upper end of Elk Flats Trail.

A4. SIDEWINDER

This trail winds through the woods (hence its name) and is probably the most challenging. From Pipeline the trail climbs uphill through the woods and intersects Lemolo Run at 0.5 mile. The challenge is to ski this first section downhill with lots of step turns. Crossing Lemolo Run, the trail goes downhill, turns left and intersects Big Buck Trail in a large opening at 0.9 mile (0.4 mile from the intersection with Lemolo Run).

A5. BIG BUCK

Big Buck Trail is a gentle downhill and level run from Lemolo Run. It initially starts in dense timber, but at 0.2 mile intersects Sidewinder (on the right) in an open area. Proceed through the open area, cross a road (the main snowmobile route to the west) and back into the trees. At 0.4 mile the trail intersects Bobtail (also on the right) in another open area. The trail drops downhill, crosses Poole Creek and connects with Elk Flat Trail in a third open area. Note: the creek crossing is only a snow bridge, so it may be difficult to cross in early fall or late spring.

A6. ELK FLATS

The Elk Flats Trail parallels the east side of Elephant Mountain Ridge. It is a downhill and level run from the intersection with Lemolo Run to the Poole Creek Campground. The trail starts where Lemolo Run crosses the main snowmobile trail adjacent to a small clearing. It runs south, intersecting with Bobtail in an open area at 0.2 mile. At 0.3 mile it crosses Poole Creek on a wooden bridge and enters a large opening at the base of Elephant Mountain. The trail then parallels Poole Creek and intersects Big Buck Trail (on the left) at 0.5 mile. It goes back into a small band of trees and then into another opening and across Poole Creek on a second bridge. At 0.9 mile the trail crosses the main highway and enters the Poole Creek Campground. Following the entrance road into the campground, it crosses the main snowmobile trail at 1.0 mile and finally connects with Poole Creek Trail at 1.2 miles.

Returning to the resort area from this point is somewhat confusing as the trail is poorly marked and there are several campground roads to follow. Your best bet is to just parallel the west edge of the lake and head north. It's only a mile to the resort from here.

A7. BOBTAIL

Bobtail trail is a short 0.4 mile connecting link between Big
Buck Trail and Elk Flats Trail. It is fairly level and goes
through two large open areas. There are some beautiful views to
the west and south.

A8. POOLE CREEK

Poole Creek Trail starts a little over 0.1 mile west of the
resort parking lot, branching to the left off the trail that
feeds into the lower end of Pipeline and Lemolo Run. It runs
south and then turns east where it crosses a snowmobile trail
from the lodge at mile 0.4. The trail then drops down in a small
canyon and crosses Poole Creek on a wooden bridge at mile 0.5.
Climbing back up the other side, it winds through trees and
coming out above the main camp ground at 0.6 mile. Here the
trail is not well marked. You can proceed either left or right
along a loop through the camp ground on one of the access roads.
The right branch ties into Elk Flat Trail at mile 0.7; the left
branch connects with a new return trail to the resort. This new
trail exits from the north end of the campground, goes through a
tunnel of trees, turns left down a steep bank parallel to Poole
Creek, and crosses it on a narrow bridge. Climbing up the other
side, it ends just below the main resort building.

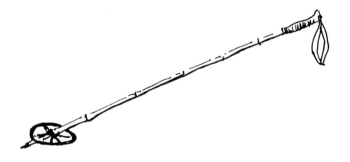

B. DIAMOND LAKE

Diamond Lake is dominated by two volcanic peaks: Mt. Bailey to the west and Mt. Thielsen to the east. Mt. Bailey, a 8363-foot high composite volcano, has several bowls or glacial cirques that are favorites of downhill skiers. Mt. Thielsen, a 9182-foot plug dome is a challenging technical climb in winter. Both have trails leading to their base.

Two major Oregon highways, 138 and 230, provide access to the area.   It is a favorite winter recreation sie for people from Medford, Roseburg and Klamath Falls, an 80 to 85 mile drive. The lodge area on the northeast side of the lake has ski and snowmobile rental, and a sliding hill for tubes.

Approximately 100 miles of cross country ski trails are available, most of them marked with the standard blue diamonds, courtesy of the Nordic Center and the Umpqua National Forest. A few in the vicinity of the resort are groomed.   Skiing is also available at nearby Crater Lake National Park and Lemolo Lake. Trail difficulty varies from beginning to advanced.   The more advanced trails are on Mt. Bailey and along the Pacific Crest trail in the newly created Mt. Thielsen Wilderness. Most trails offer beautiful views of the lake, Mt. Bailey or Mt. Thielsen. Be sure to bring your camera.

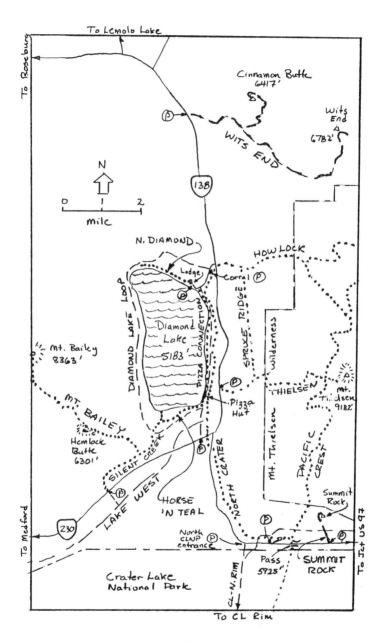

To Lemolo Lake

To Roseburg

Cinnamon Butte
6417'

Wits
End
△
6782'

WITS END

N

0   1   2
mile

138

N. DIAMOND

HOW LOCK

Lodge

Corral

P

DIAMOND LAKE LOOP

Diamond
Lake
5183'

PIZZA CONNECTION

SPRUCE RIDGE

Wilderness

Mt. Bailey
8363'

MT. BAILEY

Pizza
Hut

P

THIELSEN

Mt.
Thielsen
9182'
△

Hemlock
Butte
6301'

SILENT CREEK

LAKE WEST

HORSE
'N TEAL

NORTH CRATER

Mt. Thielsen

PACIFIC CREST

Summit
Rock

P

To Medford

230

North CLNP
entrance

P

CL-N. RIM

Pass
5925'

P

SUMMIT
ROCK

P

To Jct US 97

Crater Lake
National Park

To CL Rim

23

B1. CINNAMON BUTTE & WITS END

Trail Difficulty:	Intermediate to advanced on road
Starting Point:	Cinnamon Butte Lookout parking area, 3.7 miles north of Diamond Lake Lodge turn off on Highway 138; elevation 4820'
Trail Length:	3.0 miles (4.8 km) to Cinnamon Butte; 5.0 miles (8.0 km) to Wits End; 5.5 miles (8.8 km) to end of road; one way
Elevation Change:	1600' gain to top of Cinnamon Butte; 1960' gain to Wits End
Maps:	USGS: Diamond Lake (15 min.) USFS: Umpqua National Forest; Diamond and Lemolo Lake Nordic Trails - Umpqua National Forest

This trail requires a long steep climb in and a great downhill run out. The grade of both trails averages 10%, with some nearly level areas, and steeper portions near the summit of both peaks. Cinnamon Butte is 1.5 miles off the trail to Wits End and provides the best view of the surrounding area, especially Mt. Thielsen, Lemolo Lake, the North Umpqua Canyon, Sawtooth Ridge and Diamond Peak; thus this shorter trip is the most rewarding. Wits End is aptly named, as I thought I would never get there skiing through slow, wet, spring snow.

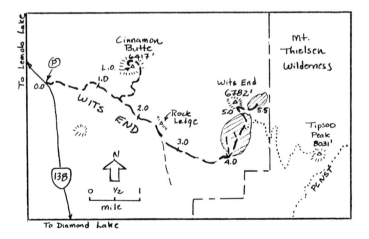

Mile	Description

Mile **Description**

0.0 Park at the Cinnamon Butte LO turnoff from Highway 138, where there is room for about 4 cars. The trail starts uphill immediately on a wide road.

The trail, on a road, goes through several broad turns climbing between 5% and 15%.

1.5 Junction with trail to Cinnamon Butte, elevation 5500'. Here the trail is level.

*   *   *   *   *   *   *   *   *

The narrow trail on the left (Road No. 4793) climbs to the top of Cinnamon Butte, 1.5 miles away. The grade is 12% with potential avalanche hazard near the top. The trail circles the east side of the butte and reaches the top from the north.

3.0 A fire lookout, on top of the butte, provides a great view in all directions.

Return by the same route - take it easy going down the trail around the butte.

*   *   *   *   *   *   *   *   *

The main road continues. A sign at the junction labels the Wits End Road (No. 100) and indicates that the Tipsoo Trail, No. 1472, is 3 miles ahead.

This trail continues on for 4.0 miles (6.4 km) at a 7% average grade. Initially it follows a side-hill providing a view to the south and of Mt. Thielsen.

2.4 The trail is just below an exposed peak and lava flow. It is a short and easy climb to the top if you wish to make this detour.

The trail continues through the trees, and is nearly level for about half a mile.

2.7 Spur No. 200 goes to the right.

4.2 The trail turns north and enters a clear-cut area. This open area provides a beautiful view west of Cinnamon Butte, Lemolo Lake and the North Umpqua River Canyon.

4.6   The Tipso hiking trail takes off to the right.
           This is a summer trail only.

           Continue uphill through the clear-cut area.

5.0   High point on the road just behind Wits End, a small
           peak to the northwest below the main ridge of Tipsoo
           Peak.   The trail turns right and drops into a
           different valley.

5.5   End of trail.

           Return over the same route - a great downhill
           run.

B2. THE PIZZA CONNECTION

Trail Difficulty:	Beginning on campground roads
Starting Point:	500 feet south of the Diamond Lake Lodge at a boat launch area; elevation 5190'
Trail Length:	2.5 miles (4.0 km) one way
Elevation Change:	20 feet along lake shore
Maps:	USGS: Diamond Lake (15 min.) USFS: Umpqua National Forest; sketch map from the Diamond Lake Nordic Center

This trail provides a pleasant trip along with east shore of Diamond Lake through a Forest Service campground. The area is wooded and provides a view of 8363-foot high Mt. Bailey to the west. The trail ends at the South Shore Pizza Hut. Numerous loop trails offer interesting variations to this trail system. The main trail is called "Mozzarella Blvd", with alternate loops called, "Olive Way", "Mushroom Alley", "Pepperoni Overpass", and "Jalapino Hill". All are marked with blue circles on metal poles and name signs, courtesy of the Diamond Lake Nordic Center.

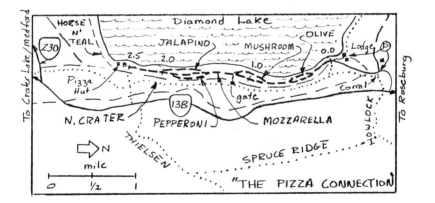

27

Access is from the Lodge area.   Walk or ski south of the lodge
past cabins near a green building on the lake shore.   Snowmobiles
may use the starting point to gain access to the cabins, so be
careful. A new parking area was recently contructed at the
junction. The North Crater Cut Off starts across the road
through a small trailer camp.

Mile	Description
0.0	Start heading south to the left of the green building and to the right of a small hill. Do not ski up on the road to the left; this is snowmobile territory.
0.3	Olive Way loop begins to the right.
0.6	Olive Way loop returns.
0.8	Mushroom Alley loop begins to the right.
1.1	Mushroom Alley loop returns.
1.3	Forest Service gate house, access to snow-mobile road to the left. This station is closed in the winter.
1.6	Pepperoni Overpass begins uphill to the left.
1.7	Jalapino Hill drops off to the right.
1.9	Pepperoni Overpass returns on the left.
2.0	Jalapino Hill returns.
2.5	The trail turns to the left and exits at the South Shore Pizza Hut.

The Mt. Thielsen Trail is to the left and
uphill, though it is not well marked. The
Horse 'n Teal Trail starts across the open
area left of the building, and turns right
around the south end of the lake. The
North Crater Trail, left across the snowmobile road and through the woods for 0.2
mile, leads back to the starting point along
the east side of the snowmobile road.

B3. NORTH DIAMOND

Trail Difficulty: Beginning on trail

Starting Point: Diamond Lake Lodge area;
                          elevation: 5200'

Trail Length: 1.6 miles (2.6 km), one way

Elevation Change: 15' along lake shore

Maps: USGS: Diamond Lake (15 min.)
                          USFS: Umpqua National Forest

   This is a short, easy trail along the north shore of Diamond
Lake, formally called the Vista Trail. Originally a hiking trail,
during the summer of 1987 it was partially converted to a paved
walking, bicycle, wheelchair and groomed ski trail. Since
construction is about half complete, the trail may be difficult
to use. There are excellent views of the lake, Mt. Bailey and
Mt. Thielsen.

   The trail begins just north of the lodge parking lot and
follows the old Diamond Lake Vista Trail (No. 1455) or Diamond
Lake Loop Trail (No. 1460), depending upon where you start.
Return over the same route or follow the loop road back past the
sledding hill and then downhill to the lodge area, about a four
mile trip. The latter part of the loop is shared with
snowmobilers.

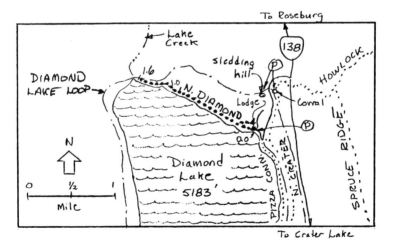

Mile	Description
0.0	Start just behind the motel building and climb the bank on the left. An alternate route is to go left through the cabin area to the end of the parking lot, climb the bank, and meet the trail at mile 0.2.
0.3	Vista Point - a good view of Mt. Bailey. Continue skiing along the lake shore through beautiful Ponderosa pine trees.
1.0	The trail drops down almost to lake level.
1.5	The trail turns into the woods.
1.6	Intersection with the Diamond Lake Loop Road at the Lake Creek bridge and campground. Turn left to continue around the lake. Turn right to return past the sledding hill and snowmobile rental area - 2.4 miles.

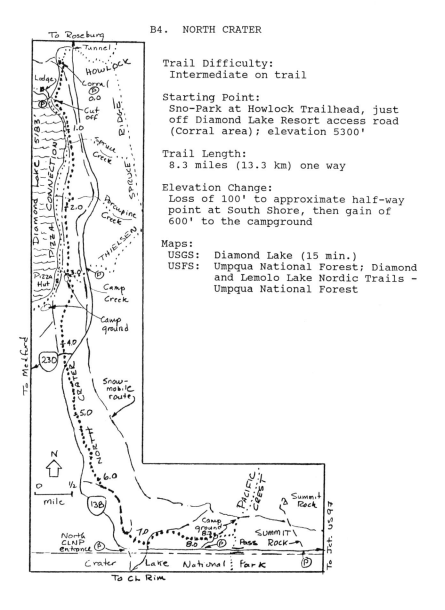

B4. NORTH CRATER

Trail Difficulty:
Intermediate on trail

Starting Point:
Sno-Park at Howlock Trailhead, just off Diamond Lake Resort access road (Corral area); elevation 5300'

Trail Length:
8.3 miles (13.3 km) one way

Elevation Change:
Loss of 100' to approximate half-way point at South Shore, then gain of 600' to the campground

Maps:
USGS: Diamond Lake (15 min.)
USFS: Umpqua National Forest; Diamond and Lemolo Lake Nordic Trails – Umpqua National Forest

This is a long north-south trail that parallels the east shore of Diamond Lake for part of the way, and crosses several of the major trails in the area. In the woods most of the way, it does not provide many scenic views, but is useful to connect with other trails. It follows a summer hiking trail marked with the standard blue diamonds and small wooden squares with carved numbers marking every half mile.

Mile	Description
0.0	Start at the Howlock Mtn. Trailhead (Corral area) where there is parking space for about six cars. This is just off the main entrance road to Diamond Lake Resort. The distances on some of the winter trail signs are wrong. Turn to the right and ski adjacent to the horse corrals. Follow a fence on the left and make a sharp left turn just before the snowmobile road.
0.3	Ski down a bank and cross a snowmobile road. Ski back into the woods and start downhill.
0.8	North Crater Cut Off. Taking this trail to the right you cross a snowmobile trail to the Diamond Lake Lodge area and the Pizza Connection trails. This trail, approximately 0.2 miles long, goes downhill, dog legs to the left, passes through a summer trailer camp, and ends at the entrance to the resort area. It is difficult to find from the other end because you must climb a bank to see the first markers.
1.3	Cross Spruce Creek.
1.5	North access to Diamond Lake Guard Station and Vistors' Center - the midpoint on the Pizza Connection Trails. It is 600' to the station.
1.7	Cross a wide straight trail.
1.9	Cross Porcupine Creek. Uphill for a short distance.
2.2	South turn off to the Diamond Lake Guard Station and Visitors' Center - the midpoint on the Pizza Connection Trails. It is 1600' to the station. Level trail for a short distance.
2.5	Downhill stretch.
2.7	Small stream crossing, then level through an open

area.

3.1	Intersection with the Mt. Thielsen Trail. It is 0.2 mile to the South Shore area (Pizza Hut) by a poorly marked and confusing trail. Each end is marked, but they do not meet in the center. To the left it is 0.5 mile to Highway 230 by a somewhat difficult and again poorly marked route that intersects the highway about 0.2 mile south of the Mt. Thielsen Trailhead. It took me three tries to find all these bits and pieces of these connecting trails. These trail markings may be removed.
3.2	Cross Camp Creek. The trail drops down into a major draw and back up the other side. The west leg of the Mt. Thielsen Trail from the South Shore terminates here.
3.5	Intersection with Trail No. 1456, the old Mt. Thielsen Trail. A large metal building is 200' to the west. Just beyond this point the trail splits - keep left.
3.6	Cross a snowmobile road and enter a large clearing. Summer hiking Trail No. 1457 also crosses here. You are now at the low point on the trail.
4.5	Cross Highway 230 about 0.1 mile west of the junction with Highway 138.
4.7	Cross Highway 138 about 0.1 mile south of the junction with Highway 230. Begin climbing parallel to Highway 138. There are no trail markers for the next mile; however you are passing through a dense Lodgepole Pine area where the trail is clear.
5.7	Drop down a small bluff, ski level for a short distance, and then ski up a narrow ridge.
6.1	Intersection with a road that was an old stock trail. Turn left and follow it. There are no winter markings only the half-mile wooden markers.
6.4	Switchback on the stock road across a stream channel.
6.8	Leave the stock trail and turn right up the north side of a draw. There is a blue diamond to indicate this junction. A steep uphill climb.
7.2	The trail levels out.
7.4	Intersect the snowmobile and cross country ski trail

from Crater Lake NP on a fire access road. It is 0.1 south to Highway 138 and the park boundary. If you take this side trail, it eventually connects to the North Entrance ski and snowmobile trail leading into Crater Lake National Park.

Proceed straight ahead (east) on the common trail.

7.7   Leave the snowmobile road and head to the right.

8.3   Enter the North Crater Campground. It is 0.4 mile south to Highway 138. This entrance is marked on Highway 138 with "North Crater Trail, No. 1410". It is 0.8 miles from the entrance to the Crater Lake National Park north entrance along Highway 138.

If you continue east through the campground, just to the left of the outhouse (sorry, too much snow to allow its use in the winter), 0.3 miles ahead is the Pacific Crest Trail. This short spur is marked with blue diamonds.

B5. HOWLOCK

Trail Difficulty: Intermediate on trail

Starting Point: Howlock Mtn. Trailhead (Corral
                         area), 0.1 mile off access road
                         to Diamond Lake Lodge (opposite
                         road to sledding hill); elevation:
                         5300'

Trail Length: 3.5 miles (5.6 km) one way

Elevation Change: Gain of 750' to junction with
                         Thielsen Creek Trail

Maps: USGS: Diamond Lake (15 min.)
                         USFS: Umpqua National Forest;
                                Diamond and Lemolo Lake Nordic
                                Trails - Umpqua National Forest

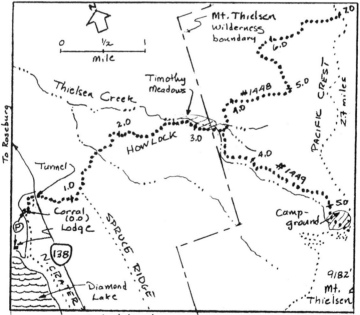

35

This is a fun trail, an easy climb through the woods and a nice
run back downhill. It also provides access to the loop trip on
Spruce Ridge, Mt. Thielsen and North Crater trails. At the upper
end, two routes that access the Pacific Crest Trail are not
marked. Howlock Trail is marked with the standard blue diamonds
in both directions to the Spruce Ridge Trail junction, and then
only uphill to Timothy Meadows.

The mileages on the blue trailhead sign are incorrect, the ones
on the summer trail signs are the correct values. This is also
the trailhead for the North Crater Trail.

Mile	Description
0.0	Parking is provided for approximately six cars at the trailhead. Be sure not to park in the private entrance for the corral. If the trail head is not plowed, you will have to park on the road to the Lodge or at the sledding hill.
	Start uphill on Trail No. 1448 - the one on the left marked with the blue diamonds. Trail No. 1448A, the Rueb Long Trail, comes back into No. 1448 about 0.1 mile uphill just before the tunnel.
0.2	Tunnel under Highway 138 - just south of the entrance to the Diamond Lake Lodge access road. The tunnel is a large culvert, about 12 feet high. You should take your skies off, especially if they are waxed, as the floor is dirt.
	Another summer trail sign on the other side - continue uphill.
1.2	Junction with Spruce Ridge Trail - marked with a blue sign. Continue down into a small draw and back uphill.
1.7	Cross another small draw.
2.5	West end of Timothy Meadows with Thielsen Creek flowing through it. The blue diamonds end. A summer trail sign on the left about 0.2 mile ahead identifies the area. For about one mile the trail is 20 feet above the south side of the meadow.
3.2	Boundary of Mt. Thielsen Wilderness area. A wooden sign is just off the right side of the trail.
3.5	Turn left and cross Thielsen Creek. Two wooden summer

trail signs are on the opposite side. One, No. 1448, is the continuation of the Howlock Mtn. Trail - it is 3.5 miles north to the Pacific Crest Trail. On the right, No. 1449, is the Thielsen Creek Trail - it is 2.0 miles south to Thielsen Camp and 2.3 miles to the Pacific Crest Trail. Both trails are narrow, poorly marked with blazes, and extremely difficult to follow in the winter. Advanced skiers can make a triangular loop using these two trails and the Pacific Crest Trail - a distance of 8.5 miles (13.7 km) and a climb of 1200'.

Return over the same route and enjoy the downhill run.

B6. THIELSEN

Trail Difficulty: Intermediate to advanced on trail

Starting Point: On Highway 138, 1.5 miles north of
                           junction with Highway 230, and 2.6
                           miles from turn-off to Diamond
                           Lake Lodge; elevation: 5300'

Trail Length: 3.5 miles (5.6 km) to Pacific Crest
                           Trail, one way

Elevation Change: 1950' to Pacific Crest Trail

Maps: USGS: Diamond Lake (15 min.)
                           USFS: Umpqua National Forest;
                                  Diamond and Lemolo Lake Nordic
                                  Trails - Umpqua National Forest

Originally the Mt. Thielsen Trail started at the South Shore of
Diamond Lake near the Pizza Hut. There is a blue winter trail
sign across the snowmobile roads from the Pizza Hut, at the
crossing of the North Crater Trail, and blue diamonds at various
points along a primitive trails. It is difficult to follow, and
the sign probably will be removed. So, unless you wish to
"timber bash" the 0.5 mile through the woods, you should start
from Highway 138. Very little, if any, parking is available on
the highway during the winter.

This trail follows hiking trail No. 1456, a popular route for
climbing Mt. Thielsen in the summer. The ski trail is well-
marked with the standard blue diamonds for 1.5 miles to the
Spruce Ridge Trail. Beyond this point, you have to depend upon
tree blazes, difficult to identify at best. It connects with the
Pacific Crest Trail just below 9182-foot high Mt. Thielsen, a
prominent volcanic plug dome.

Thielsen Trail is best enjoyed as part of a loop trip, using
Howlock, Spruce Ridge and the North Crater trails, a round trip
of 9.1 miles (14.6 km). I would prefer starting at the Howlock
Trail parking area (Corral area), and skiing the loop clockwise.

Mile   Description

0.0   Start at the east side of Highway 138. The trail
                           is marked with a summer trail sign, message board,
                           and blue diamond with a black arrow pointing uphill.

                           It is 0.5 miles downhill (across the road) to the

South Shore at the Pizza Hut. You can "timber-bash" through the woods for 0.2 mile, across a snowmobile trail, and through the woods for 0.2 mile to the North Crater Trail. A final 0.1 mile brings you to the Diamond Lake Loop snowmobile trail and the Pizza Hut at the end of the Pizza Connection Trails. A marked trail started about 0.1 miles south on the Highway at the top of a cut bank - the blue diamonds may still be up.

Start skiing uphill, winding through the trees. This trail is steeper than Howlock trail, average-ing a 10% grade.

1.5   Intersection with Spruce Ridge Trail at 6100'. It is 2.5 miles to the Howlock Trail. The blue diamonds do not continue beyond this point. Only experienced skiers should continue as it is easy to become lost. Continue uphill.

2.0   Switchback to the right and enter the Mt. Thielsen Wilderness.

3.1   Ski through two switchbacks, left and then right. You are now just below the south side of a ridge.

3.5   Intersection with the Pacific Crest Trail. You are at to the tree-line below the peak of Mt. Thielsen. It is almost another 2000' to the top.

It is 2.1 miles north to the Thielsen Creek Trail and 5.7 miles south to Highway 138 and the Crater Lake National Park boundary.

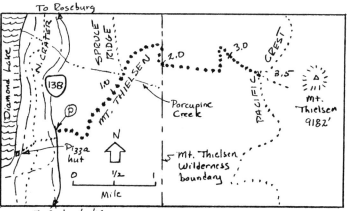

B7. SPRUCE RIDGE

Trail Difficulty: Intermediate on trail

Starting Point: Mile 1.2 on Howlock Trail; elevation
                             5650'; or mile 1.5 on Thielsen Trail;
                             elevation: 6100'

Trail Length: 2.5 miles (4.0 km), one way

Elevation Change: Gain of 450' from Howlock Trail

Maps: USGS: Diamond Lake (15 min.)
                             USFS: Umpqua National Forest;
                                    Diamond and Lemolo Lake Nordic
                                    Trails - Umpqua National Forest

Spruce Ridge Trail connects Howlock and Thielsen trails; thus
you can start from either end. It is a fairly gentle trail, with
less than a 5% grade uphill from north to south. Since it runs
parallel to the east shore of Diamond Lake, Mt. Bailey and the
lake are occasionally seen from the trees.

There are many turns and ups and downs on the trail, but
nothing difficult. The trail makes loops around the heads of
Spruce and Porcupine Creeks. I have used this trail in a 9.1-mile
(14.6-km) loop trip from the Mt. Howlock Trailhead (Corral area),
up Howlock trail for 1.2 mile, across Spruce Ridge for 2.5 miles,
down Thielsen for 1.5 mile, across Highway 138 to North Crater
Trail (0.4 mile), and back along North Crater Trail 3.5 miles.

Mile   Description

0.0   Start at the Howlock Trail junction (mile 1.2),
             marked with a blue sign. Follow the standard
             blue diamonds uphill through the trees.

1.0   Ski around the head water of Spruce Creek.

2.2   Ski around the head water of Porcupine Creek.

2.5   A blue sign marks the intersection with Thielsen
             Trail. The Thielsen Trail is only marked down-
             hill from this point.

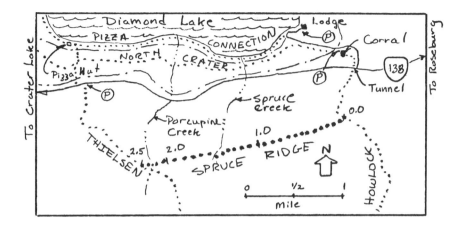

B8.   HORSE 'N TEAL

Trail Difficult:	Beginning on trail
Starting Point:	South Shore Pizza Hut; elevation 5190'
Trail Length:	1.5 miles (2.4 km) one way
Elevation Change:	10' - essentially level
Maps:	USGS: Diamond Lake (15 min.) USFS: Umpqua National Forest

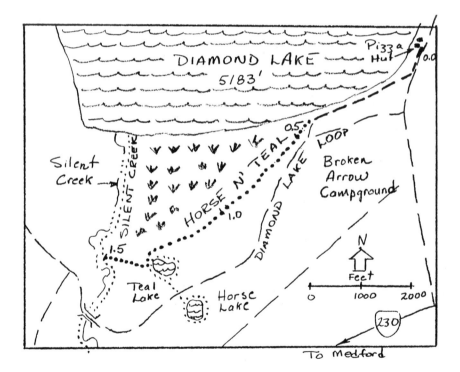

Horse 'n Teal, named after two small lakes in the area, is along the south shore of Diamond Lake. It is any easy trail that weaves in and out of the trees, along a marsh, past Teal Lake, and ends at Silent Creek. It is also the trail connecting the Pizza Connection from Diamond Lake Resort to Silent Creek Trail, the access to the Mt. Bailey Trail. It is marked with the standard blue diamonds, and some summer trail tree blazes and signs.

Mile   Description

0.0   Start at the South Shore Pizza Hut and ski south
           past the buildings on the Diamond Lake Loop road
           - a snowmobile trail in the winter - and across
           Short Creek.

0.1   Turn right at the marked trail head sign (the
           snowmobile road turns right 0.1 mile further south).
           Ski through an open area, part of the South Shore
           Campground.

0.4   Enter the trees at a point marked with a summer
           trail sign "No. 1482 - Horse 'n Teal."

0.6   Ski around the south edge of a large marsh and open
           area.

1.2   The trail goes into the trees and touches the north
           edge of Teal Lake. It then turns north and finally
           west. The summer trail also goes south around the
           west side of the lake. It is 0.4 mile to Horse Lake
           by this route.

1.5   Intersection with Silent Creek Trail and the west
           bank of Silent Creek. Turning left for 0.3 mile
           brings you to the Diamond Lake Loop Road and a
           bridge over Silent Creek; turning right 0.4 miles
           brings you to the south shore of Diamond Lake.

           You can return over the same route, or make your
           own route back to the start - all you have to do
           is head east parallel to the lake shore.

B9. SILENT CREEK

Trail Difficulty:	Beginning on trail
Starting Point:	Sno-Park on Highway 230, 2.7 miles southwest of junction with Highway 138 (Three Lakes Rd. No. 3703); elevation 5390'
Trail Length:	2.7 miles (4.3 km) one way
Elevation Change:	Loss of 200' to Diamond Lake
Maps:	USGS: Diamond Lake (15 min.) USFS: Umpqua National Forest; Diamond and Lemolo Lake Nordic Trails - Umpqua National Forest

Silent Creek flows through dense timber into the south end of Diamond Lake, and the trail follows its banks most of the way; a beautiful and easy trip. If you are careful, you may see large trout swimming in the creek as you get close to Diamond Lake. The trail is marked with the standard blue diamonds and is easy to follow.   It also provides access to Hemlock Butte and the Mt. Bailey Trail.

The trail ends at the south shore of Diamond Lake, so you must return over the same route; however, you can take Horse 'n Teal Trail to the South Shore Pizza Hut and then go north to Diamond Lake Resort, 4.5 miles (7.2 km).

Mile	Description
0.0	Sno-Park area on the north side of Highway 230 with room for approximately 15 cars. This is also an access point for snowmobile trails along the west side of Diamond Lake.
	The trail head is marked with a sign at the top of the snow bank. It heads northeast through the trees, winding with many ups and downs, but nothing difficult.
1.2	First view of Silent Creek. The trail follows along the west bank and provides some beautiful scenery.
1.5	Intersection with the Mt. Bailey Trail on the left, as marked with a sign.

1.9   Cross a small wooden bridge over a tributary to Silent Creek, usually piled high with snow.

2.0   Intersect the Diamond Lake Loop road, a major winter snowmobile route - be careful when crossing.

             Take a right across the bridge over Silent Creek, and then a left along the opposite bank of the creek.

2.3   Intersection with Horse 'n Teal Trail; it is 1.5 miles east to the South Shore Pizza Hut.

             Continue along the east bank of Silent Creek. Here you should be able to see trout. The trail winds through the woods and eventually comes out onto an open marsh area.

2.7   South shore of Diamond Lake. The trail ends, but you can ski along the shore line to the east. The mouth of Silent Creek blocks travel to the west.

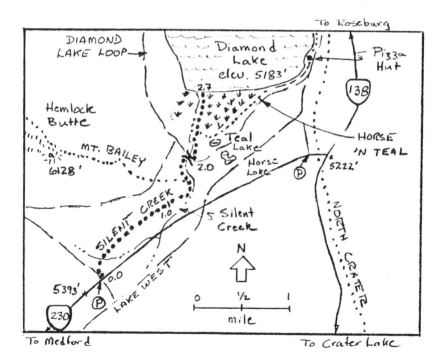

B10. MT. BAILEY

Trail Difficulty:	Advanced on trail
Starting Point:	Mile 1.5 on Silent Creek Trail; elevation 5200'
Trail Length:	5.0 miles (8.0 km) one way
Elevation Change:	800' to flanks of Hemlock Butte, and 3160' to top of Mt. Bailey
Maps:	USGS: Diamond Lake (15 min.)
	USFS: Umpqua National Forest; Diamond and Lemolo Lake Nordic Trails - Umpqua National Forest

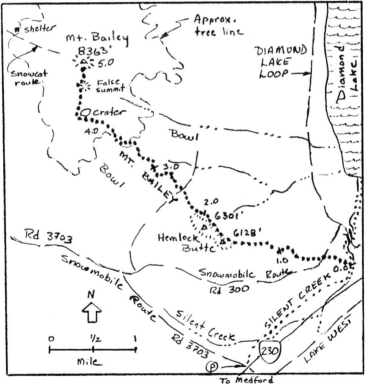

This is probably one of the most demanding ski trails in the area. The exposed area near the top of Mt. Bailey and the potential for avalanche require good preparation and extreme caution. For the experienced skier the view and the challenge of the Mt. Bailey slopes is more than worth the climb. For those who are only downhill skiers and do not wish to make the climb, a snowcat trip is available through the Diamond Lake Resort. The snowcat trip climbs the west side of Mt. Bailey and has a warming shelter at timberline.

Intermediate skiers can reach the Diamond Lake overlook on the flanks of Hemlock Butte. This short trip is protected by the trees, well-marked, and provides a view of Diamond Lake and Mt. Thielsen. Make a loop trip by intersecting the spur road at mile 2.5 and then skiing back along it and road No. 3703 to the Sno-Park, a round trip of 7.0 miles (11.3 km).

The trail is marked with the standard blue diamonds for the first 2.5 miles past Hemlock Butte to the spur road crossing. Beyond this point, there are a few blazes and the trail is difficult to follow.

Park at the Sno-Park on Highway 230, 3.0 miles west of the junction with Highway 138, and ski to mile 1.5 on the Silent Creek Trail, on the west bank of Silent Creek.

Mile	Description
0.0	Ski up the slope away from Silent Creek. The trail then winds through the woods over fairly level terrain.
0.4	Cross a snowmobile road (spur road 300). The summer trail head sign is across the road (No. 1451). The trail back to Silent Creek is signed No. 1479. On the snowmobile road to the right it is 0.4 mile to the Diamond Lake Loop Road, and an additional 0.2 mile to the Silent Creek bridge.
	Switchback across two small streams (right and and then left) on nearly level ground.
0.5	Begin climbing up the slope of Hemlock Butte at a 15% grade heading almost due west.
1.0	Switchback to the right and follow a northeast facing sideslope.
2.0	Rock overlook through the trees of Diamond Lake and

Mt. Thielsen. From here the trail is fairly level through the trees. Hemlock Butte is approximately 300 feet above the trail. Continue behind the rock outcrop.

2.5   Cross a spur road. It is approximately 1.0 mile to the left to Road No. 3703 and 3.0 miles to Highway 230. Approximately one mile to the right the road intersects the east facing Mt. Bailey bowl at the. bottom of a run. The blue diamond markers end here.

       Cross the road and look for the Mt. Bailey Trail sign (Trail No. 1451). Start climbing moderately.

2.6   A short level portion.

2.7   The slope increases to about 30% and starts through a series of switchbacks, passing several rock outcrops.

3.5   Overlook of the Mt. Bailey Bowl and view of Diamond Lake. Turn back left away from the bowl and continue uphill. You will now switchback between this bowl and another south-facing slope of the mountain.

3.8   Overlook of south-facing bowl. View south to Crater Lake rim, Mt. McLoughlin, Rogue River Valley and Hemlock Butte. Turn right and continue uphill. You are at the approximate timberline.

4.1   Overlook of main east-facing bowl. View of Mt. Thielsen and Diamond Lake. Turn left and continue uphill.

4.3   Start circling around the south and west edge of a large crater. A snow-patch in the this crater evidently has not melted in recent time. The false summit can be seen above and to the north.

4.7   False summit with a beautiful view. The trail continues north along a connecting ridge following the edge of the main east-facing bowl.

5.0   The summit of Mt. Bailey. You can ski the bowl to the southeast and intersect the west side loop road at the bottom, about three miles away, or ski down the west slope towards the warming shelter. This latter slope is the main one used by the snow-cat skiers. Beware of avalanches.

B11.   SUMMIT ROCK

Trail Difficulty:	Beginning on road
Starting Point:	Highway 138, 2.4 miles east of the North Crater Lake NP Junction, and 1.0 mile east of the Douglas-Klamath Co. Line; elevation: 5785'
Trail Length:	1.0 mile (1.6 km)
Elevation Change:	Gain of 325' to summit
Maps:	USGS: Diamond Lake (15 min.) USFS: Umpqua National Forest

This is a short, easy, unmarked trail to a small basaltic lava dome used for a quarry. A quarry road leads almost to the top; thus skiing up it is a cinch. From the top, you can see the back side of Mt. Thielsen, and the upper Klamath Marsh area. A connecting snowmobile road provides access to the Pacific Crest Trail and the North Crater Trail.

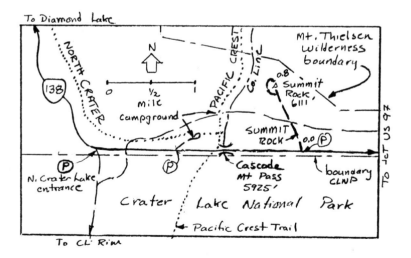

49

Mile	Description
0.0	Park on the north side of Highway 138, just below and to the east of the summit at the county line. The road is identified only by a stop sign. Parking is limited, depending upon the amount of snow plowing.
	Ski north north-west and slightly uphill.
0.4	Cross the east-west snowmobile road, marked with orange diamonds, and several red ones. Turning right takes you downhill towards Highway 97 and Diamond Lake Junction; turning left takes you uphill 0.8 miles to the Pacific Crest Trail. In another 1.0 mile, you will intersect the North Crater Trail.
	Continue north - a wooden, white arrow points to the "Federal Highway Administration Project" rock pit.
0.8	A clearing and the base of Summit Rock. It is about a 200-foot climb to the top.
	Continue uphill and switchback to the left. The quarry road circles behind the peak stopping within 30 feet of the top. You might have to climb this this last portion on foot.
1.0	Top of Summit Rock - a beautiful view.

Trail Difficulty:	Advanced on trail
Starting Point:	Highway 138 at the Douglas-Klamath County line (Cascade Mtn. Pass), or from the North Crater Trailhead campground; elevation: 5900'
Trail Length:	10.5 miles (16.9 km) to junction of Howlock Trail, one way
Elevation Change:	Gain of 1400' to Mt. Thielsen Trail, then loss of 400' to Thielsen Creek
Maps:	USGS: Diamond Lake (15 min.) USFS: Umpqua National Forest; Mt. Thielsen Wilderness; Pacific Crest National Scenic Trail (Oregon Central Portion)

This challenging trail crosses the ridge lines and slopes around Mt. Thielsen. The trail has many nearly level stretches, but also has sideslopes which may be drifted with snow. It is not a difficult trail to ski, however following it is extremely difficult. The trail, primarily for summer hiking traffic, is marked only with silver-gray diamonds, which may be at or below the snow line. I have had several frustrating experiences skiing portions of this trail. It is amazing the number of clearings that look like the trail in winter. Following this trail is slow, so allow about twice your normal skiing time. Your best guide may be Mt. Thielsen and map and compass. Current policy with the Forest Service is to remove all trail markings in wilderness areas.

You can enjoy this trail starting from the south at Highway 138 and skiing north. If you lose your way, it is easy to return to the starting point. Also, the trail can be combined with runs down Thielsen, Thielsen Creek, or finally Howlock Trails. The really ambitious mountain skier can do a winter climb of Mt. Thielsen.

Mile	Description
0.0	The Pacific Crest Trail crosses Highway 138 at the northern Crater Lake NP boundary (Cascade Mtn. Pass: elevation 5925), which is also the boundary between Klamath and Douglas counties; however,

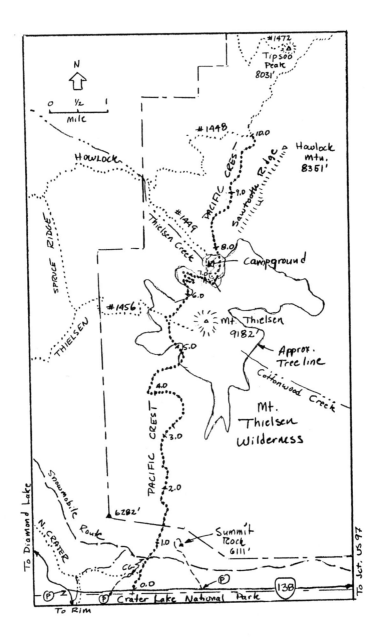

N

0   ½   1
mile

#1472
Tipsoo
Peak
8031'

#1448
Howlock

Howlock
mtu.
8351'

PACIFIC CREST

10.0

Sawtooth Ridge

9.0

SPRUCE RIDGE

#1449

Thielsen Creek

8.0

Campground

7.0

THIELSEN

#1456

6.0

Mt. Thielsen
9182'

Approx.
Tree line

5.0

Cottonwood Creek

4.0

PACIFIC CREST

3.0

Mt.
Thielsen
Wilderness

2.0

To Diamond Lake

Snowmobile Route

N. CRATER

6282'

1.0

Summit
Rock
6111'

CC

0.0

P

To Jct. US 97

P   2

P   Crater Lake National Park

138

To Rim

52

there is no parking.

Instead, it is easier to start from the the parking
area for the North Crater Trailhead. This is 0.5
mile to the west of the summit where parking is
available for about five cars. Ski 0.4 mile in on
the campground access road. At the campground, ski
north, to the left of the outhouse, and follow the
trail marked with the standard blue diamonds.
After 0.2 mile the trail intersects the Pacific
Crest Trail. From here it is 165 miles to
California and 249 miles to Washington - or so the
sign says. We have more realistic goals in mind.

You are now about 0.2 mile north of Highway 138
on the Pacific Crest Trail (PCT). One blue diamond
marker indicates the north-bound direction of the
PCT. Note: many of the summer signs use PCNST
(Pacific Crest National Scenic Trail). From here
on, the trail is marked only with the PCT silver-
gray diamonds, which are hard to find. Ski north.

0.5   Cross a snowmobile trail and enter a campground.
To the left the snowmobile trail ties into the
North Crater Trail after 1.0 mile and Highway 138
after 1.3 miles. To the right the snowmobile
trail heads downhill and crosses the Summit Rock
Trail after 0.8 mile. Continue through the trees
on a nearly level grade. Be careful, I had
difficulty following the trail here, as it is not
marked with the silver-gray diamonds for the next
0.6 mile.

1.1   Wilderness boundary; sign on right. Silver-gray
diamond markings start again.

Begin climbing on the slopes of Mt. Thielsen,
initially at 5% and increasing to 10%, through
dense woods.

2.5   The trail is on a sidehill and follows the contours
around the southwest flank of Mt. Thielsen. Enter
a southwest-facing bowl.

3.6   Head almost due west along this bowl into an open
area. Spectacular view of Crater Lake National
Park to the south including the pumice desert.
The trail is almost level from here on.

4.0   Swing around a point providing a view of Diamond
Lake and Mt. Bailey. You are still on a sidehill.
The trail goes back into the trees and heads north-

east.

4.4 Swing around another point and get a breath-
taking view of Mt. Thielsen to the northeast
across a second bowl.

The trail then goes back into the trees; across
two large talus slopes; in and out of the trees;
and finally steepens just before the Mt. Thielsen
Trail crossing.

5.7 Intersection with the Thielsen trail. It is a 3.0-
miles and a 1950-foot drop to Highway 138 near the
south end of Diamond Lake. You are now at the
high point on the trail. It is a 1850-foot climb
to the top of Mt. Thielsen - good luck.

This is the best view point on the entire trail:
Diamond Lake and Mt. Bailey to the west; Lemolo
Lake and Cinnamon Butte to the north; and on a
clear day Diamond Peak, Bachelor and Three Sisters
can be seen in the distant north.

The trail drops down from here and follows around
a third bowl. The first part is on a open talus
slope below Mt. Thielsen, and the second part is
is in the trees, climbing slightly at the end.

6.7 Ski around another point on a prominent ridge
radiating from Mt. Thielsen. Drop down and head
east on a north-facing sidehill trail.

Go through two long switchbacks and head east
again. Near the bottom there are three smaller
switchbacks.

7.6 Cross Thielsen Creek just above a large meadow.

7.8 Intersection with the Thielsen Creek Trail (No.
1449). It is a 5.8-mile and a 1600-foot drop to
the Howlock Mtn. Trailhead (Corral area) near
Diamond Lake Lodge. Thielsen campground is 0.2
mile down this trail, though the area next to
the trail is often used for camping. There are
several signs marking this junction, including
one spelled "Crek". Even though the Thielsen
Creek Trail is signed at the junction, it is
difficult to find due to the open area.

Start climbing uphill and then level out,
following the contours around the west facing
slope. You are back in dense woods again.

9.9   Start climbing again.

10.5   Intersection with the Howlock Trail (No. 1448).
               It is a 7.0-mile and a 1900-foot drop to the
               Howlock Mtn. Trailhead (Corral area) near
               Diamond Lake Lodge.

               No major trail intersection occurs further north
               until you reach the Miller Lake Trail in 5.0
               miles. Tipsoo Peak is 2.0 miles ahead; thus you
               could tie into the Tipsoo Peak Trail on the other
               side, and then ski down Wits End, past Cinnamon
               Butte to reach Highway 138. Windigo Pass is 19
               miles ahead.

Trail Difficulty:	Beginning to intermediate
Starting Point:	Various locations
Trail Length:	4.0 to 11.5 miles (6.4 to 18.5 km)
Elevation Change:	varies
Maps:	USGS: Diamond Lake (15 min.); Crater Lake National Park and Vicinity (26 x 25 min.)
	USFS: Umpqua National Forest; Rogue River National Forest; Diamond and Lemolo Lake Nordic Trails - Umpqua National Forest

Three fairly long trails in the Diamond Lake area follow
snowmobile trails, and provide easy or more challenging
experiences. The main problem is competing with snowmobiles on
parallel tracks. The three trails are described below in general
terms in increasing levels of difficulty. All except the Crater
Lake - North Rim Trail are marked with orange diamonds.

B13a. LAKE WEST

This trail starts at South Shore near the Pizza Hut and crosses
Highway 230 about 0.5 miles west of the junction with Highway
138. It runs southwest 7.0 miles (11.2 km) to Lake West in the
Rogue River National Forest and parallels Highway 230. It climbs
about 200' to the midpoint where it can be accessed from the
Silent Creek/Three Lakes Road Sno-Park. From here it is 4.0 miles
to Lake West across Highway 230. The snowmobile route continues
on parallel to the Rogue River.

A detailed trail description of the portion from the Sno-Park
and then west is found under the Union Creek section.

B13b. DIAMOND LAKE LOOP

This trail follows the loop road around Diamond Lake, a
favorate snowmobile route. However, the road is wide enough to
allow skiing on one of the shoulders. It starts at Diamond Lake
lodge, goes south between the Pizza Connection and North Crater
trails to the South Shore area (mile 2.5). It then turns west

parallel to Horse 'n Teal Trail, crossing Silent Creek and the trail by the same name (mile 4.5). It then proceeds north through the summer home area and on the lower flank of Mt. Bailey. At the north end of the lake, it crosses Lake Creek and intersects the North Diamond Trail (mile 9.0). From here it goes east past the base of the sledding hill and snowmobile rental area and then back south to the lodge. It is 11.5 miles (18.5 km) around the lake with the only elevation gain on the north end near the sledding hill (about 100').

B13c. CRATER LAKE - NORTH RIM

This trail starts at the north entrance to Crater Lake NP off Highway 138, and heads south for 9.2 miles (14.8 km) to the rim road. It starts at 5800' elevation and gains about 200' near the north edge of the Pumice Desert, about 3.0 miles in. It then drops down about 50' across the desert and back up the other side (at about 5.0 miles in). Here it climbs steadily between Red Cone and Grouse Hill to the rim at 7250' elevation (1450' above the starting point). Snowmobiles are not allowed beyond this point. The view of the Lake and to the north is spectacular.

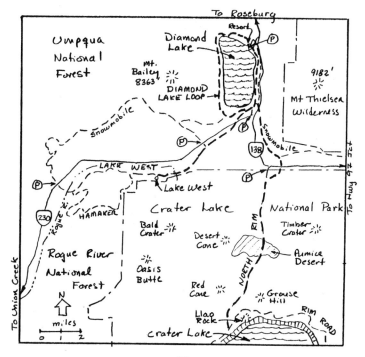

C. CHEMULT

Volunteers in Chemult have started a program of cross country ski instruction for the area children and adults. In cooperation with the Forest Service, the volunteers have set and groomed a number of ski trails behind the Chemult Ranger District complex of the Winema National Forest. Five to six miles (8 to 10 km) of tracks in the woods and on logging roads were developed during the winter of 1986/87. Plans are to sign and intermittantly groom these trails during the winter of 1987/88.

These trails are located to the north of the Miller Lake Road and start from the north end of the Ranger District complex. They follow spur Roads No. 100, 109, 080, 083 and 020 as shown on the map on the next page. The maximum elevation gain is 100 feet. Check with the Ranger District (address in the Appendix) for more details.

A longer unofficial trail used for a number of years leads into Miller Lake. This is approximately a 24-mile (39-km) round trip to Digit Point campground on the south side of the lake. USFS Road No. 2731 starts about one mile north of Chemults and heads west towards the Cascade Crest, with about a 1000' gain in elevation over the 12-mile trip. For a diversion about half way in, climb Deer Butte, a 500-foot high cinder cone about one-half mile south of the road.

A shorter, beginning level trail goes into Corral Springs. This four-mile (6.5-km) round trip begins about three miles north of Chemult and heads west over Forest Service Road No. 9774. This fairly level trip, with only one hill, has a historical interest. According to early journals, explorers and military expeditions stopped at the springs. In 1843, John C. Fremont, Kit Carson and others may have camped here during exploration of the area.

The springs are about 0.2 mile north of Road No. 9774, at the north end of the campground. They flow from the bottom of a pumice deposit enclosed by a rail fence.

Snowmobiles also use portions of the Miller Lake and Corral Springs Roads. An alternate route to Corral Springs is to follow the Corral Springs Loop (spur Road No. 112) or Cresent-Chemult Express (spur Road No. 110) snowmobile routes from the Forest Service complex.

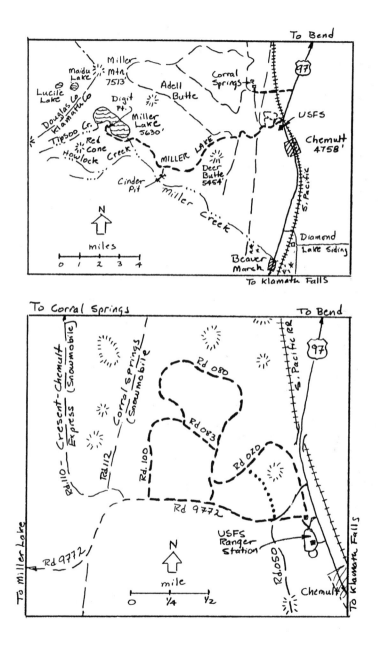

D. CRATER LAKE NATIONAL PARK

Crater Lake National Park is the best cross-country skiing area in southern Oregon. The Park covers more than 250 square miles, with over 100 miles of trails. The terrain varies from 4300 feet at the south entrance to over 8900 feet at the top of Mt. Scott; the rim road is over 7000 feet. The high elevation provides skiing conditions that surpass most other areas in the Cascades; often it is the only place to ski when snow is sparse elsewhere.

The average accumulative snowfall is 550 inches (over 45 feet), with 14 feet on the ground in late winter. Driving into the Park you are impressed by the high snowbanks that may persist even into July. It is a place of extremes - brilliant sunny skies and warm temperatures to raging blizzards and bitter cold. On a clear day, the view of the lake and a short ski trip along the rim are unforgettable. Winter is my favorite time at Crater Lake.

The rim drive is closed in the winter; however access is available from the south by Highway 62, either from Klamath Falls or Medford. Snowmobilers have limited access from the north entrance, south of Diamond Lake, to the rim road. Often the road from the Headquarters area to Rim Village is closed by an over-night storm. The Park Service is good about plowing the roads, and will usually have the rim access road open by mid-morning or noon. Parking, information and restroom facilities are available at the new Steel Center in the Headquarters area. Parking, cafeteria, gift shop and restrooms are available at Rim Village. Skiing equipment can be rented at the cafeteria-gift shop. No camping or gas facilities are provided in the winter.

Rangers patrol the back country, and a volunteer ski patrol serves the park trails on weekends. None of the trails is groomed; however most are marked with signs and blue diamonds or orange tags. The rim road is not marked, but it can be followed part way by the orange snowplow poles that mark the edges of the pavement. Avalanches can be a problem, so observe the signs at key locations. Free permits required for back country camping are available at the Steel Center. Snow and weather conditions can be obtained by calling the Headquarters (phone number and address listed in the Appendix).

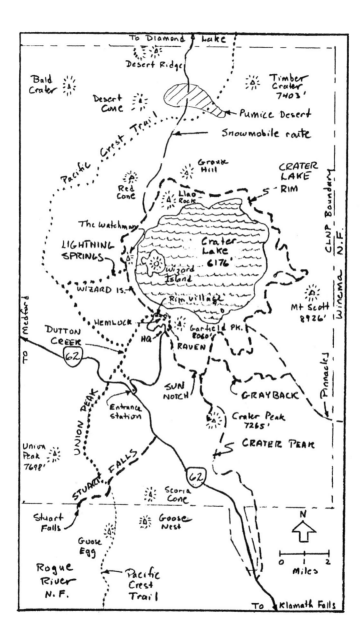

D1. HEMLOCK

Trail Difficulty:	Beginning to intermediate along trail
Starting Point:	Rim Village parking lot; elevation 7100'
Trail Length:	1.5 miles (2.4 km) in a loop
Elevation Change:	Gain of 50 feet; then loss of 100 feet
Maps:	NPS sketch map available at Headquarters

Close to the Rim Village, this fun trail starts from the east end of the parking lot just to the right of the rest room. Climb the bank and ski downhill across an open area to an opening in the woods. The trail is marked from here with blue diamonds. It winds through the woods and climbs a small ridge. At the end of the ridge the trail either descend through an open area to the right, or down a steep hill to the left. The road from Headquarters to the rim is below and to the right - thus you cannot get lost. The steep hill can be traversed very nicely. At the bottom of the steep hill is a large open area just below the Lodge. Ski back towards the Lodge and then left through the woods to the beginning.

Many open areas invite play and telemarking, especially the large open bowl area below the Lodge. Here are gentle and steep slopes for practice. On a clear day the entire Klamath Basin can be seen to the south. It is a beautiful place to play and get some sun.

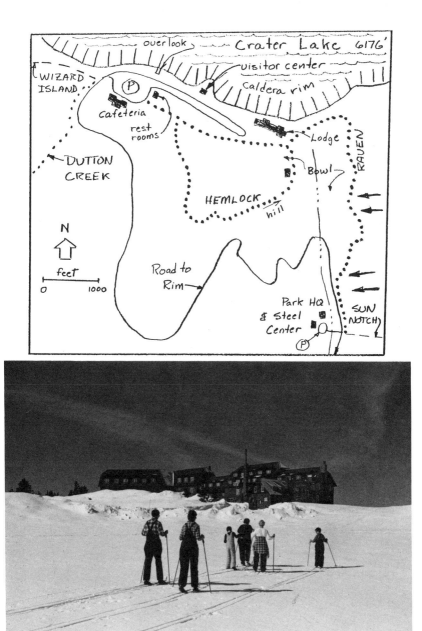

D2.   RAVEN

Trail Difficulty:	Advanced on trail
Starting Point:	Just east of the rim Lodge; elevation 7070'
Trail Length:	1.0 mile (1.6 km) to Headquarters
Elevation Change:	Loss of 590 feet.
Maps:	USGS: Crater Lake National Park and Vicinity (26 x 25 min.) NPS: Crater Lake

This is one of the steepest trails in the Park, but fun for advanced skiers to run from the rim to Headquarters through a Hemlock forest.   Numerous switch-backs are in the upper section, and several avalanche paths cross the lower section. Intermediate skiers can traverse or snowplow down the steeper portions.   The original road to the Lodge and the route of the original Crater Lake Ski Race followed approximately this route.

The trail starts approximately 150 yards to the east of the Lodge on the rim.   Do not ski too close to the rim as snow overhangs may be dangerous.   A sign marks the beginning of the trail, and blue diamonds the trail itself.   It initially descends steeply through numerous switch-backs and stays on the east side of a small valley just below Castle Crest ridge.   Near the bottom, the trail levels out and crosses several potential avalanche paths, marked with orange warning signs.   The last portion parallels the east side of the road from Headquarters to the rim.   The end of the trail is opposite the entrance to the Headquarter's parking area and also marked.   The lower end of the trail connects to the Sun Notch Trail.

See Hemlock Trail for a detailed trail map.

D3. WIZARD ISLAND

Trail Difficulty:	Beginning on road
Starting Point:	Rim Village parking lot: elevation 7070'.
Trail Length:	2.3 miles (3.7 km) to Wizard Island overlook - one way
Elevation Change:	Gain of 100'
Maps:	USGS: Crater Lake National Park and Vicinity (26 x 25 min.)
	NPS: Crater Lake

This is the most popular trail in Crater Lake National Park. On a clear day the view is fantastic and the route easy. In bad weather it can be difficult to find the trail, much less see the lake. The trail follows the rim road and is fairly level, with an occasional up and down. Watch for views of the lake about every three-quarters of a mile. Some geologic formations visible along this trip are Wizard Island, a recent cinder cone; Llao Rock, a dacite lava flow filling a glacial valley; Mt. Scott, the highest point in the park; and distant Mt. Thielson, a plug dome near Diamond Lake.

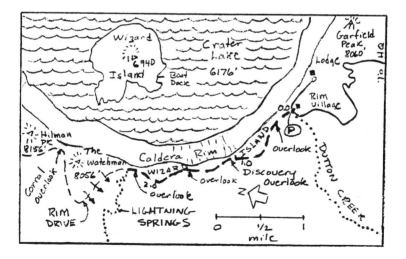

The snack bar, gift shop, rest rooms at Rim Village are places
to get out of the cold. Several other beginning and advanced
trails such as Hemlock, Dutton Creek and Raven begin at or near
Rim Village.

Mile   Description

0.0   Start from the rim village parking lot, where
                  space for over 100 cars is available. Walk to
                  the west where the rim access road enters the
                  lot, and climb the snow bank. Point your skiis
                  parallel to the lake edge to prevent them from
                  inadvertently sliding over the edge.

                  Start down hill parallel to the rim. Don't be
                  discouraged by this first hill, probably the
                  most difficult on this trail. This wide-open
                  area also lets you practice downhill techniques.

0.3   Low point and a view of the lake. Continue behind
                  a protective hill. Union Peak is seen to the south.

1.0   A second overlook of the lake (Discovery Point).
                  The small draw to the left is a good area to
                  telemark or just have some fun. Climb uphill and
                  behind a second protective ridge.

1.6   Ski downhill to a third overlook. This area
                  consists of a wide open meadow where many practice
                  telemarking or just plain downhill running. Climb
                  uphill behind another protective ridge. Platey
                  andesite lava is to the right side of the
                  road cut.

2.3   Ski downhill to the Wizard Island overlook.
                  0.1 mile is the start of the Lightning Springs
                  Trail. A campground and overlook area are in
                  the trees to the upper right.

                  From here the trail goes around The Watchman to the
                  Corral Overlook. This section can be extremely
                  difficult if the snow is drifting. The roadway
                  can be completely covered creating a steep slope
                  and a long way to the valley below.

                  Return by the same route.

D4. SUN NOTCH

Trail Difficulty:	Beginning to intermediate on road
Starting Point:	On access road to the rim across from the Park Headquarters buildings: elevation 6480'
Trail Length:	4.5 miles (7.2 km) one way
Elevation Change:	Gain 635' to Sun Notch, with one intermediate hill and valley
Maps:	USGS: Crater Lake National Park and Vicinity (26 x 25 min.)
	NPS: Crater Lake

This is one of the two most popular trails in the Park, especially if the weather is bad on the rim. Starting 600 feet below Rim Village, it is protected by the ridge-line behind Garfield and Applegate Peaks. Many times the rim road is closed after recent snow fall, leaving this one of the few places to ski in the Park. The trail follows the rim road from the Park Service housing area, with spectacular views of Sun Creek Valley, Dutton Ridge and Vidae Falls. Unfortunately, the only view of Crater Lake is from Sun Notch, at the end of this trail.

Even though the trail is classified as beginning to intermediate , there are many slopes above and below the road that provide challenges to the advanced skiers. There is also a potential avalanche problem below Applegate Peak near Sun Notch; however, there is an alternate trail.

Mile	Description
0.0	Parking is available for approximately 10 cars on the east side of the rim access road across from the summer service station area. If this is full, another parking area is on the west side in the Headquarters area, about 0.1 mile ahead. Information and rest rooms are available here.
	Climb the snow bank on the east side of the road and ski downhill adjacent to the Park Service housing area.
0.5	Low point on the trail. Start the long uphill climb at about 5.0%. Just remember the nice long run you will have on the return.

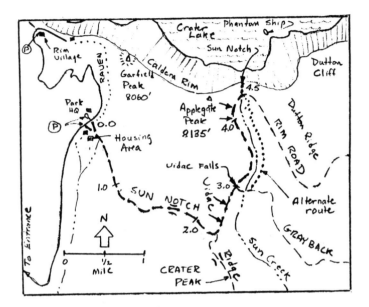

1.8 Finally - the pass. You are now at elevation 6790',
    310' above the start, and 410 above the low point.

    Start downhill, enjoy the view and take some time to
    have fun skiing down some of the side slopes.

2.3 Junction with the Crater Peak Trail. Crater Peak is
    2.5 miles south.

    Continue around the andesite lava road cut on the left
    and look down into Sun Creek Valley and Meadow. Dutton
    Ridge is across the valley. Watch for small avalanche
    areas on the left.

3.0 Vidae Falls on the left. It may be difficult to see
    in the winter due to snow and ice, but the water can
    can be heard running under the road. You are again
    at a low point, elevation 6530'. The Grayback Motor
    Nature Road takes off to the right, the main road
    continues around to the left.

    About 0.5 miles ahead, the main road leaves the trees

and is exposed to the potential avalanche hazard from Applegate Peak. If an avalanche hazard exists, then follow the Grayback Road down to Sun Meadow, 0.2 miles away and then ski up the center of the meadow. This results in a steep uphill climb (not marked) through the trees at the upper end, but is far safer.

If no avalanche hazard exists, proceed up the main road to the left, initially in the trees and then on an exposed and wind sculptured side slope.

4.3   The road curves around the bottom on Sun Notch. Leave the road and continue uphill through the trees and into an open area. The alternate from Sun Meadow crosses the road here but is not marked.

4.5   Sun Notch with a beautiful view of Crater Lake. Several overlooks, the one uphill and to the north provides a view of Phantom Ship. Take care near the edge; its a long way down to the lake. You are now at 7115', 585' feet above the low point at Vidae Falls.

Return by the same route.

D5. DUTTON CREEK

Trail Difficulty:	Advanced on trail
Starting Point:	Rim Village, just south of Rim Road; elevation 7050'
Trail Length:	2.4 miles (3.9 km) to Pacific Crest Trail; then 2.1 miles (3.4 km) to Highway 62 or Annie Springs on entrance road
Elevation Change:	Loss of 980 feet to Pacific Crest Trail; then gain of 260 feet to saddle
Maps:	USGS: Crater Lake National Park and Vicinity (26 x 25 min.)
	NPS: Crater Lake

The upper part of this trail zig-zags down through old growth Mountain Hemlock. It is marked with the standard blue diamonds and major switchbacks with black or white arrows on the diamonds. The route parallels Dutton Creek, part of an old wagon road used to reach the rim. It is named for the Chief of the USGS party which sounded the Lake in 1886. The latter half of the trail follows the Pacific Crest Trail to either Highway 62 or to Annie Springs near the entrance station. This section circles the head-waters of Castle Creek and then climbs a steep ridge to a saddle where the trail splits. The two routes drop slightly in the last half mile.

This trail is probably the most difficult in the Park; however an intermediate skier can snowplow or traverse down the steeper sections. It is fairly well marked and easy to follow. Make arrangements to return to the Rim Village; hitch-hiking will sometimes work. A ski race followed this route a number of years ago - the fastest time was around 30 minutes; however, under normal conditions the trip takes about three times this long.

Mile	Description
0.0	Park at Rim Village. Walk to the start of the Rim Road (Wizard Island Trail), then ski south along the west bank of the road from Headquarters and watch for the blue diamonds. About 200 yards south, the trail begins to drop away from the road and descends steeply through the trees along numerous switch-backs.

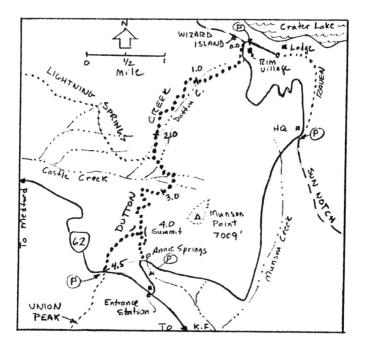

1.2   The trail flattens and enters some small meadows surrounded by Lodgepole Pines.

2.4   Junction with the Pacific Crest Trail at Dutton Campground. An orange winter sign marks this intersection. The Lightning Springs Trail is to the right. Turn left and follow the nearly level trail. It is marked with blue diamonds, orange and red rectangles and the summer trail silver-gray diamonds. The latter may be buried below the snow line.

         The trail curves around to the right, crossing several tributaries of Castle Creek.

3.5   Begin the steep climb to the saddle. Note several older "X-C" yellow wooden trail signs used in this area.

4.0   At the saddle, marked with another orange winter sign, the trail divides. Highway 62 is to the right, and Annie Springs straight ahead.

         If you ski straight ahead:

After skiing level for a short distance, the trail descends steeply along the left side of a small valley. Several switch-backs bring you down to the left of a water tank and onto a portion of the old entrance road.

4.5　　Junction with the entrance road just to the left of the bridge over Annie Springs (named after Annie Gaines, the first woman settler to see Crater Lake and descend to the shore). The entrance station is about 100 yards to the right. Parking is available across the road.

or.... if you turn right at the saddle:

This is the continuation of the Pacific Crest Trail. Climb up a small rise and then descend to the left through the trees along a side-hill. After about a quarter of a mile, the trail turns sharply right and levels out.

4.5　　Junction with Highway 62, 0.9 miles west of the entrance road to the rim. A turn-out provides parking for approximately five cars.

D6. LIGHTNING SPRINGS

Trail Difficulty:	Intermediate to advanced on trail
Starting Point:	Mile 2.5 on the Wizard Island Trail (Rim Road); elevation 7170'
Trail Length:	4.0 miles (6.4 km) to Pacific Crest Trail; 8.2 miles (13.2 km) to Dutton Creek Trail
Elevation Change:	Loss of 1300 feet to Pacific Crest Trail, then gain of 200 feet to Dutton Creek Trail
Maps:	USGS: Crater Lake National Park and Vicinity (26 x 25 min.) NPS: Crater Lake

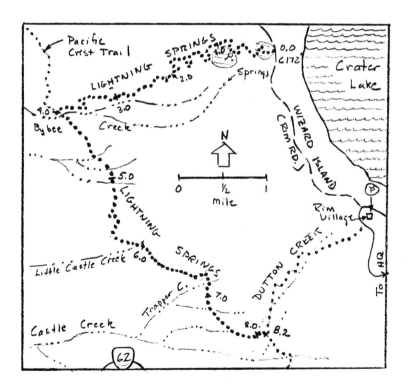

This trail is evenly divided into two unique parts. The more difficult averages 6% downhill switchbacking through open meadows near the top and into denser timber near the bottom. The second part is nearly level through timber along the lower slope of former Mt. Mazama. I have been apprehensive about skiing this trail due to reports of its steepness and the difficulty in following the trail markers. However, I was pleasantly surprised that neither was true, and in fact the trip was enjoyable. The upper part of the trail is dominated by Mountain Hemlock and Shasta Red Fir, and the lower portion by Lodgepole Pine.

The entire trail is marked with small orange and red rectangles attached to trees. They are orange on the side going downhill and red on the other. I found that the orange side was easier to see. Near the beginning of the steep portion some switchbacks are marked with the standard blue diamond and black arrow. On the Pacific Crest Trail silver-gray diamonds are used for hiking and may be buried below the snow line.

This trip is approximately 13 miles (21 km), starting at the Rim Village and ending at Highway 62 or at Annie Springs on the entrance road. This requires transportation back to Rim Village, though I have hitch-hiked back. An alternate is to return by the steep Dutton Creek Trail to Rim Village.

Mile	Description
0.0	Start on the left side of the Rim Road at mile 2.5, about 100 yards past the Wizard Island Overlook. An orange winter sign marks the start of the trail.
	Look for the orange and red metal rectangles attached to trees. Head northwest and downhill across an open area. Watch for switchbacks, some of which are marked with blue diamonds and black arrows. The first one will be to the left.
1.0	The trail goes along the north side of a large open area. Stay in the tree-line. If in doubt, remember that the trail has a fairly gentle gradient; it is never steep like Dutton Creek or the Raven Trails. Union Peak can be seen due south, a sharp point on the skyline.
2.0	The trail becomes slightly flatter from this point to the Pacific Crest Trail. Bybee Creek Valley will always be to the south (left) of the trail.
3.0	Begin to closely parallel Bybee Creek and enter

Lodgepole Pine timber.

4.0   Intersection with the Pacific Crest Trail. In deep
snow this junction will be difficult to identify.
It is nearly a right-angle intersection and only
marked for summer hiking traffic with a three-foot
high sign - difficult to see in six feet of snow.

The trail continues to the left, marked by both the
orange and red metal rectangle and the Pacific
Crest Trail silver-grey diamonds. If you inadvert-
ently follow the trail to the right, you will find
only the latter diamonds. The diamonds will be
near the snow-line, about six feet above the
ground, the rectangles at eye height or above.

Because the Pacific Crest Trail follows an old fire
access road, a wide opening through the trees
identifies it.

4.1   Cross Bybee Creek, named after an early pioneer who
operated a ferry on the Rogue River near Medford.

5.5   Start climbing slightly and go through a switchback
that may be hard to find when it abruptly turns back
to the left.

The trail then becomes narrower and goes through
denser timber.

6.0   Cross Little Castle Creek.

7.0   Cross Trapper Creek. The trail enters a more open
area. It is easy to lose the trail here.

8.2   Junction with the Dutton Creek Trail at the Dutton
Campground. This intersection is marked with a
large orange winter sign.

From here it is 2.4 miles (3.9 km) to the left up the
Dutton Creek Trail to Rim Village (a 960-foot climb
in elevation). Ahead 2.2 miles (3.5 km) is either
Highway 62 or Annie Springs on the entrance road.

Trail Difficulty:	Intermediate on road
Starting Point:	Mile 3.0 on the Sun Notch Trail; elevation 6530'
Trail Length:	4.8 miles (7.7 km) one way
Elevation Change:	Gain of 245' to midpoint, then loss of 805' to Lost Creek Campground
Maps:	USGS: Crater Lake National Park and Vicinity (26 x 25 min.)
	NPS: Crater Lake

This trail follows the gravel Grayback Motor Nature Road from Vidae Falls to Lost Creek Campground. It is seldom used in the winter, so be prepared to break trail. The middle portion of the trail is just below an exposed ridge, offering spectacular views to the south. The 800-foot drop from the high point to Lost Creek campground provides a fast downhill trip through many switch-back turns; however, remember you must climb back up this same hill. In poor weather this ridge can be cold, and drifting snow make the road difficult to follow. No trail markers are provided.

To ski this trail, start from the Headquarters area and ski up the Sun Notch Trail 3.0 miles to Vidae Falls. The Grayback Trail turns to the right. Under normal condition, you must return over the same route. This route is also used for trips around the rim to avoid the dangerous side-slopes at Dutton Ridge and near Kerr Notch. From Lost Creek Campground you can also ski down towards the old east entrance to see the Pinnacles (spires of ash, pumice and scoria cemented together by hot gases); or ski up to Kerr Notch for a good view of Phantom Ship.

Mile	Description
0.0	Start at Vidae Falls on the Sun Notch Trail. Ski right and down to Sun Meadow, about 50 feet lower. The road makes a long switchback right and then turns left. You can short-cut this by skiing down the left bank at the first turn; lots of fun in deep snow. Proceed directly across the meadow.
0.4	Start climbing through a switch-back and ski south around the end of Dutton Ridge. The trail is only moderately steep here, and begins in the trees.

1.5 The trail comes out of the trees on an exposed
    sidehill just below the ridge line. On a clear
    day you will have a beautiful view to the south.
    Maklaks Pass between Sun and Sand Creeks, is one
    mile south.

2.3 High point on the trail at elevation 6776'. Start
    downhill and back into the trees. The trail goes
    through a number of switch-backs with an average
    grade of 8.0%.

4.0 Cross Wheeler Creek.

4.7 Cross Lost Creek and enter Lost Creek Campground.

4.8 Intersect with the road from Kerr Notch to the
    Pinnacles.

    From here it is 3.0 miles (4.8 km) downhill to the
    Pinnacles (510' elevation loss), and 3.1 miles
    (5.0 km) uphill to Kerr Notch and the main rim road
    (780' elevation gain).

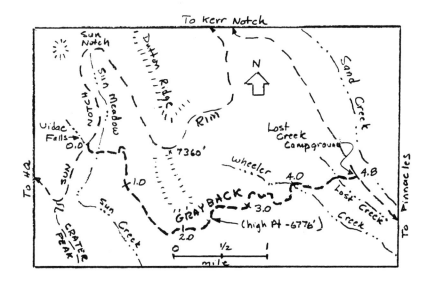

D8. CRATER PEAK

Trail Difficulty:	Advanced on trail
Starting Point:	Mile 2.3 on the Sun Notch Trail; elevation 6670'
Trail Length:	2.5 miles (4.0 km) to Crater Peak; 11.0 miles (17.7 km) to south entrance of the Park
Elevation Change:	Gain of 595' to the top of Crater Peak; loss of 2329' to south entrance of the Park
Maps:	USGS: Crater Lake National Park and Vicinity (26 x 25 min.) NPS: Crater Lake

Skiing to the top of Crater Peak is an interesting side trip from the Sun Notch Trail. The most difficult part of the trip is the climb and descent from the actual peak, a cinder cone. A large crater at the top provides shelter from the wind, and the rim a 360 degree view, including the southern part of the park and the Klamath Basin.

The trail also continues south along a fire road to the south entrance of the park. This trail follows the east bank of Annie Creek, but unfortunately is poorly marked.

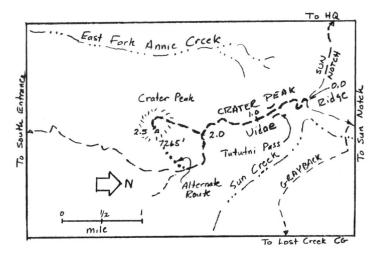

| Mile | Description |

0.0   Start from mile 2.3 of the Sun Notch trail as marked with a trail sign. The trail initially descends through a series of switchbacks, marked with the standard blue diamonds; however, it is difficult to follow the actual path. As long as you stay on the ridge line between Sun Creek and the East Fort of Annie Creek you are heading in the correct direction.

1.0   Tututni Pass, the low point in the trail - approximately 150' below the starting point.

2.0   The base of Crater Peak. The summer trail leads around to the right, but it is difficult to find. An alternate route is to ski around to the east and climb the east flank. In either case numerous switchbacks are required, as the flanks have a 40 percent slope.

2.5   Top of Crater Peak

* * * * * * * *

Beyond the Peak the trail proceeds south to the south entrance of the Park. It follows an old fire road that approximately parallels Annie Creek. It is not marked and crosses several open areas, making it difficult to follow. It exits just south of the south Park entrance on a Forest Service road. I have not skied this trail, thus can only provide sketchy information. It is 8.5 miles (13.7 km) to the south boundary of the park, and 11.0 miles (17.7 km) to the south entrance from the Sun Notch Trail.

D9. CRATER LAKE RIM

Trail Difficulty:	Advanced on road
Starting Point:	Rim Village; elevation 7070'
Trail Length:	28.9 miles (46.5 km) from Rim Village clockwise around to Headquarters
Elevation Change:	Maximum elevation at Cloud Cap: 7700'; minimum elevation at Headquarters: 6480'
Maps:	USGS: Crater Lake National Park and Vicinity (26 x 25 min.)
	NPS: Crater Lake

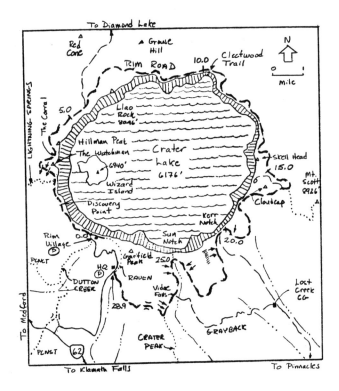

This trip is a challenging one, especially if the weather is poor. If the weather is good, the trip will be one you will never forget. Most skiers travel the rim in a clockwise direction, as this is the easiest. The trip normally takes two to three days, but it could take longer if storms develop. On a prepared trails the record for the rim trip is six and a half hours set in the late 1960's by John Day, Franco Nones, Guido De Florian and Bill Pruitt.

There are no shelter, so be prepared to camp in the snow. Because snow and weather conditions can change quickley, good equipment and preparation are a must. Snow fall can be heavy, requiring extensive trail breaking. Fortunately the trail is usually broken from Rim Village to Wizard Island overlook and from Headquarters to Sun Notch, 6.5 miles (10.5 km) of the trip.

The road can be hard to follow, so a map and compass are necessary. Avalanche conditions sometimes require long detours. The three avalanche and steep side-slope areas to be avoided are (1) around The Watchman on the west side, (2) on either side of Kerr Notch, and (3) on either side of Sun Notch. These areas may require dropping into the valley, skiing around the hazard and then climbing up the other side.

The required backcountry permit is available at Headquarters in the Steel Center, from 8 to 5 daily. You cannot obtain the permit through the mail or in advance of the trip.

Mile   Description

0.0   Start from the Rim Village parking lot. A special
               parking area has been set aside for skiers staying
               out overnight. A registration box is located at the
               beginning of the trail to the west of the parking
               lot.

               The Wizard Island trail description will provide
               additional information on the first part of the
               trip.

1.0   Lake overlook at Discovery Point

1.6   Lake overlook and wide open meadow area.

2.2   Wizard Island overlook. The Lightning Springs trail
               takes goes left about 0.1 mile ahead. Start the
               climb around The Watchman. This section can be
               difficult, especially if the road is drifted.

3.8   Corral overlook, easily identified by the log

fences. One of the best views of Wizard Island.
Continue to climb beyond this overlook.

4.4   View point to the north. You will see Red Cone,
           Bald Crater, Desert Cone, Mt. Bailey, Mt. Thielsen
           and glimpses of Diamond Lake. Start descending
           to the north entrance.

5.5   Lake overlook and view of Llao Rock. If the rocks
           on the right are not covered with snow, you will
           be able to see some glacial striations.

5.9   North entrance junction. Don't be surprised if
           you see snowmobilers; they are allowed to use the
           north entrance road to this point. Start uphill
           to the right.

7.0   Top of the long climb behind Llao Rock. The trail
           levels out and then starts downhill.

8.5   Bottom of hill and lake overlook. The trail is
           relatively flat through this section, with over-
           looks at mile 8.6, 9.2, 9.6 and 9.8.

10.1   Lake overlook and lowpoint, start uphill again.

10.3   Cleetwood Cove trail, with the parking area on the
           left - identified by the new fiberglass restrooms
           poking through the snow. Continue climbing.

10.6   The Cleetwood Flow overlook, the trail then climbs
           around Mazama Rock.

11.3   Top of the long grade.

11.7   Overlook.

12.2   Palisade Point overlook, the trail starts uphill
           and behind Roundtop.

12.8   Top of grade.

13.1   Wineglass overlook. Start uphill again.

13.7   Two overlook.

14.4   The large overlook at Skell Head - view of Mt.
           Thielsen to the south. The trail then climbs
           away from the lake, making a large loop towards
           Mt. Scott.

15.0   View of Mt. Scott.

16.0   View back towards upper Klamath Marsh.

16.3   Finally, the top of the long, long uphill climb.
        Ski around a large loop to the right at the bottom
        of the Mt. Scott bowl. The trail head is 0.4 miles
        ahead, but will be difficult to locate in the deep
        snow. It is easy to get lost here if foggy or snowy.

16.9   This is the high point on the trip: elevation 7700'.
        The dead-end road to Cloudcap overlook takes off
        to the right. Stay to the left; the second part
        of the "Y" comes in about 0.1 mile ahead. Start
        downhill to Sentinel Rock.

18.3   Redcloud Cliff and Castle Rock overlook, go uphill
        slightly.

18.6   Victor View overlook.

18.8   Sentinel Rock and a view of the lake. The trail
        again loops away from the lake to Anderson Bluffs.

19.7   Start the descent to Kerr Notch. Drifting snow,
        icy conditions and/or avalanche hazard may
        require dropping down to Kerr Valley, crossing
        the Pinnacles road, and climbing the other side.
        In extreme conditions take the Grayback Trail
        to Vidae Falls (see trail description elsewhere).

20.6   Kerr Notch and a view of Phantom Ship. The actual
        overlook is behind the trees.

20.7   Turnoff to Lost Creek Campground and the Pinnacles.
        The campground is 3.1 miles downhill and 5.9 miles
        to the Pinnacles. Start climbing to Dutton Ridge.
        Again watch for avalanche hazards.

22.5   View of the Klamath Basin.

23.3   Top of grade and view of Union Peak.

24.0   Dutton Ridge: drifting snow, icy conditions and/or
        avalanche hazard. Again it may be necessary to
        leave the trail, drop down to Sun Meadow and
        rejoin the trail at Vidae Falls.

24.6   Sun Notch. The climb of 0.2 mile through the
        woods above the trail will reward you with a
        view of the Lake. The trail continues downhill
        under Applegate Peak, another avalanche hazard.

Refer to the Sun Notch trail description for
more details of this portion of the trip.

25.9   Vidae Falls and the intersection with the Grayback trail. This is a low point; start uphill.
Watch for avalanche hazards on your right.

26.6   Junction with the Crater Peak trail, just past
an andesite lava road cut on the right.

27.1   Top of the climb. It is all downhill from here
to Headquarters.

28.9   I lied, there is a small uphill grade at the very
end (0.5 mile). There is also a side trail to the
right through the trees. Intersection with the
rim access road. The Headquarters area and the
Steel Center are 0.1 mile ahead.

From here it is 2.8 miles by road to the Rim
Village parking lot, or 1.5 miles by the Raven
Trail (described elsewhere). Since it is about
a 600' climb to the rim, you may wish to hitch
a ride, or leave a second car at the overnight
parking area at Headquarters.

Be sure to check in with the Park Service at
the end of your trip.

D10. UNION PEAK

Trail Difficulty:	Intermediate on old fire road
Starting Point:	State Highway 62, 0.9 miles north west of Annie Springs entrance station junction; elevation 6175'
Trail Length:	5.1 miles (8.2 km) one way
Elevation Change:	Gain of 375' to approximate midpoint, then loss of 260' to Stuart Falls Trail
Maps:	USGS: Crater Lake National Park and Vicinity (26 x 25 min.)
	NPS: Crater Lake

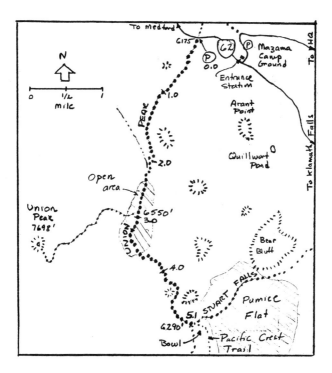

This trail, running almost due south, is just to the west of
the Klamath River and Rogue River watershed divide. It is also
the Pacific Crest summer trail. Portions of the trail provide
views of Union Peak and several other rocky knobs. The first
third of the trail is through dense forest, the middle portion
across open meadows, and the last portion through small valleys
and long the side of ridges.

The trail ends at mile 2.9 on the Stuart Falls Trail. If you do
not return over the same route, you can loop back along this
trail to Highway 62, for a total of 8.0 miles (12.9 km). Make
arrangements for a ride back up Highway 62 to your starting
point, a distance of about 3.5 miles.

Mile   Description

0.0   A turnout is plowed out on the north side of Highway
            62, with space for about 8 cars.

            The trail starts across the highway to the south,
            marked with a winter ski trail sign. The trail itself
            is marked with the standard blue diamonds; however,
            the Pacific Crest Trail silver-gray diamonds may be
            visible near the snow line.

            The trail is almost level through the trees and easy
            to follow.

2.0   The trail turns to the left and switch-backs up the
            hill at a fairly steep grade. This turn-off can be
            easily missed.

2.4   End of the steep climb and switch-backs. The trail
            enters a long north-south clearing; stay to the
            center or right side. Trail markers are few and
            far between for the next two miles. Do not turn
            off to the left along a number of side clearings.
            Eventually you will see the orange winter trail sign
            standing in the snow at the south end of this
            clearing, marking the side trail to Union Peak.

2.9   Intersection with the trail to Union Peak. Union
            Peak, to the west through the trees, is 2.6 miles
            (4.2 km) away by trail. A winter climb to the 7698-
            foot top requires experience and skill.

            You are now at the high point, elevation 6550 feet.

Continue straight ahead where you will see several blue diamonds south at a tree line. Cross several other clearings divided by narrow tree lines.

3.6   The trail turns to the left, leaves the last large clearing and descends moderately through sparse timber.

4.4   The trail enters a narrow valley, and diamonds may be difficult to locate. Several steep downhill runs are encountered.

5.0   Climb up the right side of a small ridge and circle to the left at the top.

5.1   Intersection with the Stuart Falls Trail on the north side of a large bowl. This intersection is also marked with an orange winter trail sign stuck in the snow. Continuing downhill to the right leads to Stuart Falls, 2.9 miles (4.7 km) away; and turning to the left and proceeding uphill for a short distance leads back to Highway 62, also 2.9 miles (4.7 km) away. This latter trail is mostly flat or downhill, thus making it an easy trip out. Some trail markings are difficult to find when skiing in this direction.

D11. STUART FALLS

Trail Difficulty:	Intermediate and advanced on fire access road
Starting Point:	State Highway 62, 7.0 miles north of Crater Lake NP south entrance; or 2.8 miles south of Annie Spring entrance; Cold Springs turnout; elevation 5830'
Trail Length:	5.8 miles (9.3 km) one way
Elevation Change:	Gain of 460' to half-way point, then loss of 790' to falls
Maps:	USGS: Crater Lake National Park and Vicinity (26 x 25 min.) NPS: Crater Lake

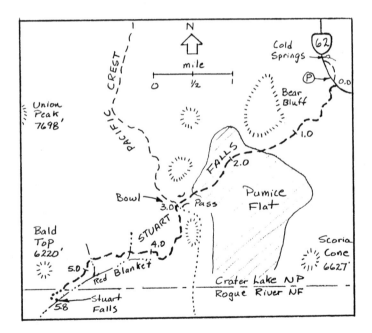

One of my favorite, this trail is used little but offers a variety of terrain plus protection from the wind which may plague the rim route. For an enjoyable short trip to a large bowl, ski to the half-way point where your can play, practice down-hill runs and telemarking, and eat lunch. The half-way point is also the intersection with the Pacific Crest Trail, part of a longer loop trip.

The trail follows an old fire access road, the latter half the original Pacific Crest Trail. For the most part it is in Lodgepole Pine and Hemlock woods, exposed only at the pass and bowl. If there is new snow, trail breaking can be somewhat tiring and difficult; however the experience is well worth the effort.

The trail is marked with the standard blue diamonds with small white triangles, and occasionally with small orange rectangles. The latter half of the trail (the old Pacific Crest Trail) is also marked with small silver-gray diamonds. The last 0.4 mile of the trail is in the Rogue River National Forest (Sky Lake Wilderness Area), and marked only with double blazes on trees.

Mile	Description
0.0	A turnout is plowed out on the east side of Highway 62, providing space for about 6 cars. Access to the trail is gained by climbing the snow bank on the west side of the road. The Park Service normally scoops out an access ramp in the snow.
	After climbing the bank, ski south 200 feet along the edge of the bank to the trail head. The trail then loops in a counterclockwise direction, crossing a powerline and climbing slightly. Look carefully for the trail markers.
	The trail then climbs gradually through a series of curves in the Lodgepole Pine and Hemlock forest. The large cinder cone that dominates the horizon to the east is 7265-foot high Crater Peak (seen when returning).
1.7	Exit the dense forest and start across the Pumice Flat. This is a fairly level area with scattered Lodgepole. A steep ridge parallels the trail on the right (northwest). It is easy to lose your way in this area, so watch for the trail markers.

2.6   The trail branches as indicated by the two blue
      diamonds. The one straight ahead follows a broad
      valley to the pass and is poorly marked. The one
      to the right is the shorter and climbs the face
      of the ridge. Both reach an open area and the
      pass at the same point. I prefer taking the right-
      hand route.

2.9   The pass and half-way point at elevation 6290'.
      Just beyond here is the intersection of the
      Pacific Crest Trail, marked with an orange sign
      (5.1 miles north to Highway 62 and 2.9 miles
      to Stuart Falls).

      A large open bowl for downhill skiing. This is
      one of my favorite spots for lunch. From one of
      high points on the bowl, you can glimpse Union
      Peak to the northwest.

      Before skiing on, remember that it is almost
      an 800-foot climb back out from the falls -
      a long and tiring trip at the end of a day.
      The trail continues down to the left (due
      south). Initially the trail is fairly level,
      but then drops sharply through the woods. This
      is one of the more difficult runs.

4.1   Cross a small stream.

4.4   Exit onto a more open and level area, paralleling
      the stream on the right bank.

5.4   End of the fire access road and the south boundary
      of Crater Lake National Park. Enter the Rogue River
      National Forest by dropping down the hill, crossing
      Red Blanket Creek, and climbing up the other side.

      The trail is difficult to follow from here. Ski
      parallel to the right bank of the stream. Keep the
      National Park Service (NPS) boundary signs on your
      right. The trail is level for several hundred
      yards before descending steeply through the trees.
      The trail is narrow with numerous switch-backs.
      Watch for the double blazes on the trees. Keep left
      around the small hill. The bottom of the falls is
      at the base of this hill.

5.8   Stuart Falls. Enter through the campground and
      turn left. The falls are approximately 40 feet
      high and may be ice and snow covered. Be careful
      not to break through the ice and snow into the creek.

E. UNION CREEK

The Union Creek Resort area is located on Highway 62 (The Crater Lake Highway) approximately 54 miles northwest of Medford and 16 miles west of the Annie Creek Junction in Crater Lake National Park. A cafe, store and cabins are located at this historic resort area near the junction of Union Creek and the Rogue River. It is built on the Crater Lake Trail used by the early pioneers crossing the Cascades. A little over a mile north on Highway 62 is the intersection of Highway 230, following the Rogue River for 24 miles to Diamond Lake. These routes are open all winter; thus Union Creek becomes an intermediate stopping point for skiers travelling from Ashland, Medford and Grants Pass to these other ski areas.

Low elevation, slightly over 3300', limits the days with good snow conditions for the Union Creek Trail system. Two other trail systems: Thousand Springs, about 10 miles west of Union Creek on Highway 62, and Lake West, about 13 miles north on Highway 230, are at higher elevation (4000' - 6000') with better snow conditions. However, they are shared with snowmobilers. These trails have been laid out and marked in cooperation with the Rogue River National Forest (Prospect District), the Grants Pass Nordic Club, and the Rogue Snomobile Club. Other trails are being planned, but have not yet been completed.

There are four parking areas on Highway 62 providing access to two trail systems, one a Union Creek Resort, one a mile north, then two on the way to Crater Lake National Park, three and seven miles respectively from the Resort. The Sno-Park about one mile north of Union Creek is a snow play area with sledding hills, outhouses, and shelter with fireplace and picnic tables. The Sno-Park at Thousand Spring has recently been enlarged and paved. The Sno-Park for the Lake West Trail is three miles west of the junction near Diamond Lake (Highways 230 and 138) on Highway 230 (Silent Creek Trailhead).

In addition to the marked trails, there are many possibilities for wilderness tours into the Rogue-Umpqua Divide Wilderness. This area, lying to the west of Highway 230 and the Rogue River, can be accessed by any number of Forest Service roads. The snow level and condition will determine how far you can travel into the area. The Forest Service has a map for this wilderness.

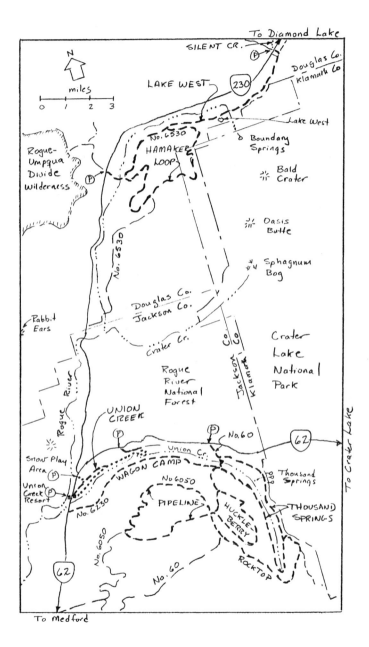

E1. UNION CREEK

Trail Difficulty: Beginning to intermediate on road and trail

Starting Point: 1) Behind the Union Creek Store, elevation
                        3320'; 2) At the Farewell Bend Sno-Park,
                        0.9 mile north of Union Creek, elevation
                        3400'; or 3) On Highway 62, 2.0 miles east
                        of Highway 230 junction, elevation 3685'

Trail Length: 4.1 miles (7.2 km) along Union Creek, one
                        way, and 3.2 miles (5.1 km) of connecting
                        trails, one way.

Elevation Change: 365' gain on trail along Union Creek

Maps: USGS: Prospect (15 min.)
                        USFS: Rogue River National Forest;
                        Trail guide from Prospect Ranger
                        District

   The Union Creek trail system has three access points, all along
Highway 62. The actual trail along Union Creek is intermediate in
difficulty, narrow in spots, with some sharp curves and fallen
logs to negotiate. All the other trails are beginning level.
Below 4000', snow may be marginal, requiring a detour around bare
spots, or avoiding some trails. The trailhead at the Farewell
Bend Sno-Park just north of the Union Creek Resort area has a
shelter with fireplace and restrooms. All trails are marked with
the standard blue diamonds.

Mile   Description

0.0   Start at the Sno-Park, 0.9 mile north of Union Creek.
                Ski east through the trees and into a large clearing
                with sledding hill, shelter and outhouses. This is
                the Farewell Bend Snow Play Area.

0.1   The actual trail starts to the east and behind the
                shelter - marked by a sign. The map on the sign
                differs slightly from the actual trail locations.
                Ski south on a nearly level trail (an old skid road).

0.6   Trail junction on improved logging road - marked
                with several blue signs.

                The right branch goes to Union Creek Resort, 0.6
                mile to the southwest. It intersects the trail
                along Union Creek just before the resort. This

trail winds through the trees, crosses a large
clearing and then makes a sharp left turn. Highway
62 parallels the trail to the west.

The left branch goes southeast and then turns south
to meet the trail along Union Creek 1.3 miles away.
The trail is generally level, with one short downhill
run. Be sure to watch for the right turn to Union
Creek, as the road continues beyond this point. From
here you can either ski up or down the trail along
the north bank of Union Creek.

*   *   *   *   *   *   *   *   *   *

0.0   Starting behind the Union Creek Resort (at cabin 21),
         you can ski up the more difficult trail along the north
         bank of the creek. Along this trail you can enjoy old
         growth Douglas Fir, waterfalls and quiet pools.

0.1   The trail from the winter play area comes in on the
         left (1.2 miles away). Just ahead the summer trail
         crosses Union Creek on a wooden bridge. Stay on the
         north bank. The trail winds through the trees and
         tall grass.

2.0   Intersection with the east branch of the trail from
         the winter play area (1.9 miles away).

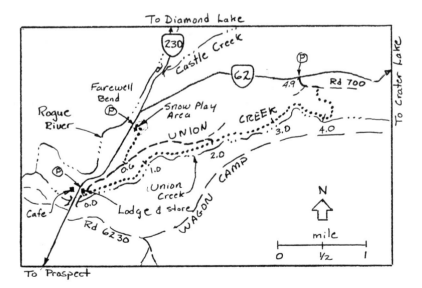

4.1   The trail turns left and leaves the creek. Ski north
           and through a level area.

4.3   Start uphill on a steep sidehill trail.

4.5   Level out and intersect spur road No. 700. This is
           the summer trail head for the Union Creek Trail, No.
           1035 - marked by a large sign.

           Depending upon snow conditions, you may have to end
           your trip here and return over the same route, or have
           someone meet you. If there is sufficient snow, turn
           left on the logging road.

4.6   Road junction - keep right and head north. This road
           is nearly level.

4.9   Intersection with Highway 62 (MP 59.3), 2.0 miles
           east of the junction with Highway 230. A blue winter
           sign, high up on a tree reads: " Union Creek Trail
           - Sno-Park 8 km", referring to the winter play area
           five miles away. Parking is limited here.

E2. THOUSAND SPRINGS

Trail Difficulty:	Intermediate on road
Starting Point:	Sno-Park on Highway 62, 5.9 miles east of junction with Highway 230 and 2.0 miles west of Crater Lake National Park boundary; elevation 4400'
Trail Length:	13.6 miles (21.9 km) in a loop
Elevation Change:	Gain of 1000' at half-way point
Maps:	USGS: Prospect (15 min.) USFS: Rogue River National Forest; Trail guide from Prospect Ranger District

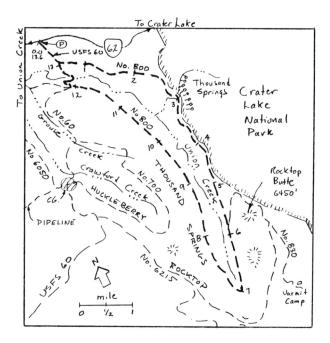

This trail is primarily used by snowmobilers; however it is occasionally used by cross country skiers. It is part of a large system of trails that start from this Sno-Park. Two main sights on the trail are the Thousand Springs area and the headwaters of Union Creek. Trail maps are available in a box at the Sno-Park.

Mile	Description
0.0	Park in the Sno-Park on the south side of Highway 62, where there is room for 50 cars. Ski south on USFS Road No. 60 on a level grade.
0.4	Junction with spur No. 900 to the left. From this point you can ski either clockwise or counterclockwise around the loop. Turn left to ski clockwise and start slightly uphill.
1.5	Spur road to the left - keep right and ski parallel to Crater Lake NP west boundary.
2.8	Summit, start downhill.
3.0	Cross bridge over stream from Thousand Springs.
3.1	Entrance to Thousand Springs parking area on left. Thousand Springs is just inside CLNP and approximately 0.2 mile east. The entire area is swampy with no definite trail.
	Continue south on the road, climbing slightly.
3.7	Cross a small creek.
4.8	Open area.
5.3	Slight downhill and view west across Union Creek to the return road.
5.8	Junction with road to Rocktop, spur No. 800. Continue south climbing on a gentle grade.
7.0	Cross springs feeding Union Creek at its upper end. You are now at the high point: elevation 5400'. Turn north and head downhill.
	The trail follows the west side of the valley at a fairly constant and long downhill run.
12.1	Junction with roads No. 60 and 6230. Turn right on No. 60 and start climbing.

12.4   Top of grade - start steeply downhill.

12.6   Cross Union Creek and climb uphill again.

12.9   Top of grade - road is fairly level from here on.

13.2   Junction with spur No. 900, your original route.
        Keep left back to Highway 62.

13.6   Sno-Park on Highway 62.

E3. ROCKTOP

Trail Difficulty:	Intermediate to advanced on road
Starting Point:	Mile 5.8 on Thousand Springs Trail; elevation 5100'
Trail Length:	10.4 miles (16.7 km) in a partial loop
Elevation Change:	Gain of 900' at approximate half-way point.
Maps:	USGS: Prospect (15 min.)
	USFS: Rogue River National Forest; Trail guide from Prospect Ranger District.

This trail is primarily used by snowmobilers; however it is occasionally used by cross country skiers. It is part of a larger trail system starting from the Sno-Park on Highway 62, 7.0 miles east of Union Creek Resort. Reaching the highest point in the system, this trail offers some spectacular views. It also connects with the trail to Varmint Camp and Red Blanket. To complete a loop from the Sno-Park requires a 17.7 mile (28.5 km) trip, including part of the Thousand Springs Trail.

Mile	Description
0.0	Start at mile 5.8 on the Thousand Springs Trail (5.8 miles south of the Highway 62 Sno-park). Climb steeply to the northeast on spur road No. 800. Be careful in this first section as the outside slope is very steep.
0.8	Switchback to the right and get the first view of Rocktop, a volcanic plug 6450' high.
1.0	Top of grade - you are now heading southeast on a nearly level grade.
1.6	Junction with spur No. 830 on the left, leading downhill for 2.0 miles to Varmint Camp and the start of Trail No. 1070 to Red Blanket.
	Continue uphill on the road to the right.
2.1	View of Union Peak to the east in Crater Lake NP.
2.4	View of the country to the southeast.

3.1   Top of grade - ski level for a short distance.

3.5   View to the north, down into the headwaters of Union
        Creek. Start uphill again.

4.7   Spectacular view to the north of Crater Lake rim and
        Mt. Thielsen.

4.8   High point on the trail at elevation 6000'. View to
        the west and southwest including Ginkgo basin. Start
        steeply downhill.

4.9   Junction with Road No. 6215. The road to the left
        eventually reaches Highway 62 near the Mommoth Pines
        area, 13 miles downhill. Take the right branch and
        ski downhill. Huckleberry Mountain, elevation 6370'
        is on the immediate right and uphill.

7.0   Junction with Road No. 60. The road to the left also
        leads to Highway 62 about 11 miles away. Ski right
        and slightly uphill. The trail shortly becomes nearly
        level and winds between large Douglass-Firs.

7.5   Cross a cattle guard.

7.8   Enter Huckleberry Mountain Campground.

7.9   A large "Y" intersection with Road No. 6050, the Pipe-
        line Trail, and spur road No. 700 (unmarked), the Huckle-
        berry Trail. Turn right and continue on Road No. 60,
        crossing a second cattleguard and heading downhill.

8.1   Spur No. 710 on the right. Continue around to the right

8.2   Cross Crawford Creek, climb uphill for a short distance,
        and then downhill again.

8.9   Cross Grouse Creek on a bridge. The junction of spur
        No. 700 is on the other side. This is the other end
        of the Huckleberry Trail. Turn left and continue
        downhill.

        The trail follows the east slope of Crawford Creek Basin
        and goes steeply downhill.

10.4   Intersection with roads No. 6230 and 800, the return end
        of the Thousand Springs Trail. It is 1.5 miles back to
        the Sno-Park on Highway 62 along the Thousand Springs
        Trail.

E4. HUCKLEBERRY

Trail Difficulty:	Intermediate on road
Starting Point:	Forest Service Road No. 60, 3.0 miles south of the Highway 62 Sno-Park; (mile 8.9 on Rocktop Trail); elevation 5190'
Trail Length:	4.7 miles (7.6 km) in a partial loop
Elevation Change:	Gain of 950' at saddle near half-way point
Maps:	USGS: Prospect (15 min.) USFS: Rogue River National Forest; Trail guide from Prospect Ranger District

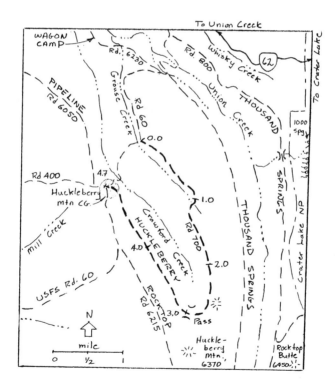

This is another trail primarily used by snowmobilers, but occasionally by cross country skiers. It is part of a larger trail system that starts from the Sno-Park on Highway 62, 7.0 miles east of Union Creek Resort. At the top of the loop around Crawford Creek Basin, there are good views of Crater Lake National Park to the north and of the Rogue River drainage to the southwest. A loop from the Sno-Park requires a 11.7 mile (18.8 km) trip, including parts of Rocktop and Thousand Springs trails.

Mile	Description
0.0	Start at mile 8.9 on the Rocktop Trail on Road No. 60. Facing southeast, take the left branch, spur No. 700. Ski uphill on the northeast side of Grouse Creek.
1.0	Switchback to the right and cross the headwater of Grouse Creek - then switchback to the left and continue uphill.
3.0	The top of the climb at a saddle - elevation 6140'. Huckleberry Mountain is due south about one half mile and Crater Lake rim and Mt. Thielsen can be seen to the northeast.
	Start downhill to the northwest at a 5% grade - the road narrows and follows a ridge.
3.9	View to the southwest of Ginkgo Basin - the grade increases to around 10%.
4.5	Cross a cattle guard and enter Huckleberry Mountain Campground.
4.7	Junction with roads No. 60 and No. 6050 (mile 7.9 on the Rocktop Trail). If you are skiing this trail in the counterclockwise direction, Road No. 700 is not marked - but enters this large "Y" intersection on the south side.
	It is 1.0 mile along Road No. 60 back to the starting point, and an additional 3.0 miles back to the Sno-Park.

E5. PIPELINE

Trail Difficulty: Intermediate on road

Starting Point: Huckleberry Mountain Campground,
                           at junction of roads No. 60 and
                           6050 (mile 7.9 on Rocktop trail),
                           4.0 miles from Highway 62 Sno-Park;
                           elevation 5460'

Trail Length: 9.9 miles (15.9 km) in a loop

Elevation Change: 980' loss from high point to turn-
                           around point at the lower end

Maps: USGS: Prospect (15 min.)
                           USFS: Rogue River National Forest;
                                  Trail guide from Prospect
                                  Ranger District

   Pipeline, not to be confused with a trail by the same name at
Lemolo Lake, is named after a water line supplying a Forest
Service warehouse near Union Creek. Primarily a snowmobile trail,
it is used occasionally by cross country skiers. This is the
lowest trail of a system starting from the Sno-Park on Highway
62, 7.0 miles east of Union Creek resort, and the only one that
you have to ski uphill to return to your starting point.   To
finish a loop from the Sno-Park requires a 17.9 mile (28.8 km)
trip, including part of the Rocktop and Thousand Springs trails.
At the lower end turn-around point, you are only 3.0 miles from
Union Creek Resort.

Mile   Description

0.0   Start at the Huckleberry Mountain Campground road
           intersection and ski west on Road No. 6050.   Ski
           downhill.

0.3   Junction with spur No. 400 - the other leg of the
           loop. You can ski either direction at this point -
           the description will proceed clockwise. Ski straight
           ahead on spur No. 400, the left branch.

0.4   Cross a cattle guard. Start uphill.

0.5   Spur No. 480 on the right. The grade becomes steeper.

0.8   Spur No. 475 on the right.

1.1	High point on loop at elevation 5650'. Start downhill.
1.4	Spur No. 468 on left.
1.8	Spur No. 460 on left - this is a major "Y" in the road.
1.9	Low point - start uphill. Hunting camp on right.
2.1	Spur No. 450 on left - trail on level grade.
2.7	Spur No. 270 on left - connecting west to Road No. 6050.
3.1	Open area on right - start downhill again.
3.7	Junction with Road No. 6050. This is the low point on the loop at elevation 4670'. This turn around point is marked with orange diamonds. Turn right and ski steeply uphill on Road No. 6050.
4.0	The trail becomes nearly level.
5.0	Junction with spur No. 510 on right. Start uphill again.
5.5	Junction with spur No. 520 on right. Slight uphill grade.
5.8	Major junction with spur No. 550 on right. Turn left past stop sign.
6.3	Spur No. 600 on left. Start uphill again.
6.6	The trail becomes nearly level.
7.0	Spur No. 700 on left.
7.5	Stream crossing on bridge and spur road on left.
8.0	Spur No. 800 on left.
9.1	Large burn area on left.
9.4	Cattle guard crossing - begin uphill again.
9.6	Junction with spur No. 400 on left - your original route.
9.9	Junction with road No. 60 and Huckleberry Campground, the starting point. It is 4.0 miles back to the Sno-Park on Highway 62.

E6. WAGON CAMP

Trail Difficulty:	Intermediate on road
Starting Point:	Junction between roads No. 6230, 60 and spur No. 800 (mile 10.4 on Rocktop Trail), 1.5 miles south of Sno-Park on Highway 62; elevation 4520'
Trail Length:	7.7 miles (12.4 km) one way
Elevation Change:	Loss of 1200' to junction with Highway 62 at Union Creek Resort
Maps:	USGS: Prospect (15 min.) USFS: Rogue River National Forest; Trail guide from Prospect Ranger District

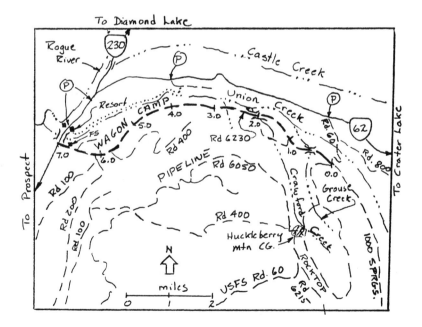

This trail is at a low elevation; thus snow cover may be
limited or non-existent on the lower portions. Primarily a
snowmobile trail, it is sometimes used by cross country skiers as
a one way link between the Sno-Park on Highway 62, 7.0 miles east
of Union Creek Resort and the resort itself. The trail uses part
of the Thousand Springs and Rocktop trails, adding an additional
1.5 miles from the Sno-Park. The trail parallels Union Creek.

Mile	Description
0.0	Junction of road No. 60 and 6230, and spur No. 800, 1.5 miles south of the Sno-Park on Road No. 60. Ski west and downhill on Road No. 6230.
0.7	Cross Grouse Creek. Wagon Camp hunter camp is to the right on Union Creek.
1.5	Spur No. 800 on left. Enter a large clearing providing a view northwest of Rabbit Ears.
2.5	Cross Crawford Creek.
	The road follows a narrow canyon on the left and is on a side-hill for the next few miles.
4.8	Cross a small canyon with a large, open logged area on the left. The road is uphill for about 0.2 mile and then is nearly level to Highway 62.
6.4	Spur No. 400 on left.
6.8	Spurs No. 100 and 300 on left - a major intersection.
7.4	Cross a water pipeline.
•7.5	Cross a cattle guard.
7.6	Forest Service warehouse area on right.
7.7	Junction with Highway 62. Union Creek Resort is 0.2 miles north on this highway.

E7. LAKE WEST

Trail Difficulty:	Intermediate on road
Starting Point:	Sno-Park on Highway 230, 3.0 miles west on junction with Highway 138 (Diamond Lake Junction); elevation 5390'
Trail Length:	8.8 miles (14.2 km), one way
Elevation Change:	Loss of 1240'
Maps:	USGS: Diamond Lake (15 min.); Garwood Butte (15 min.) USFS: Rogue River National Forest; Trail guide from Prospect Ranger District

Paralleling the Rogue River, this trail is shared by cross country skiers and snowmobilers; however the latter traffic is light. There is access to the trail from both ends, but starting from the east, you can enjoy a downhill trip. Due to the low elevation, part of the west end may not have enough snow. In either case, make arrangements for a shuttle back to the start, or you will have an 8.8 mile return trip. One benefit of this trip is the rest room and shelter at Lake West, constructed by the Forest Service and the Grants Pass Nordic Club.

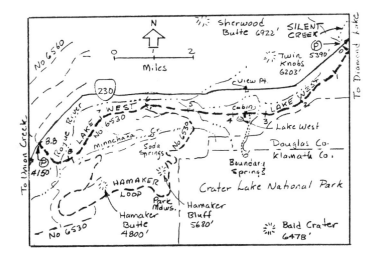

107

The trail is marked with orange diamonds, but it is not difficult to follow. There are several short steep runs which can be negotiated by snow plowing. The first half of the trail is on a narrow winding spur road (No. 760) and the second half on a wide main Forest Service access road (No. 6530).

Mile   Description

0.0   Park in the Sno-Park on the north side of Highway
            230. This is also the starting point for the
            Silent Creek Trail and the Three Lakes Snowmobile
            Trail. Parking is available for about 10 cars.

            Cross the road to the trail marked for snowmobiles
            and ski south through the woods. An alternate route
            starts 0.2 mile west on the highway where a spur
            road connects to the Lake West road. There may be
            limited parking on the highway.

0.2   Junction with the Lake West road. It is 3.2 miles
            to the left to the South Shore area of Diamond Lake.
            Turn right and head southwest.

0.4   Junction with the spur road to Highway 230 (0.2 mile
            to the north) - the alternate access to the trail.
            The trail is fairly level through this section.

3.1   Steep downhill section to stream crossing.

3.2   Cross the Rogue River. A trail to Boundary Springs
            takes off along the west side of the river. Start
            uphill.

3.5   Top of climb and trailhead for the Boundary Springs
            Trail No. 1057. It is 1.0 mile south to the springs,
            the headwaters of the Rogue River. This is a
            beautiful trip, following the west bank of the Rogue
            River. This trail intersects the one from mile 3.2,
            0.1 mile south across a small draw. The trail then
            follows the river high on the west slope of a canyon.
            At the springs area are several waterfalls and
            rapids. The trail is marked with double blazes.

            Continue on the road, heading slightly downhill.

3.9   Lake West on the left. There is a large open area
            on the right, and slightly ahead on the rise to the
            right is an outhouse with raised floor. If you head
            down to the lake and then bear around to the left, you
            will find a short trail to the winter shelter, an

18' x 18' log cabin with open front, earth floor and pot belly stove. It is for use by all winter travellers, so please take care of it, and clean up before you leave. This is the Taylor Cain Shelter.

Climb a short hill and continue west.

4.0   Top of hill and beginning of level section.

4.4   Start steep downhill section.

4.8   Bottom of hill - cross Mazama Creek. Climb up the other side. The trail is slightly downhill from this point.

6.0   Here you have two choices: (1) continue straight ahead on the road and down a steep section to Road No. 6530, or (2) turn left on the snowmobile trail through the woods to Road No. 6530 - the easier route. We chose to turn left.

6.1   Intersection with Road No. 6530, turn right. The road to the left is the Hamaker Loop Trail. Ski west on No. 6530, a road about twice as wide as the one you have been skiing on.

6.2   Junction of spur No. 760 (the alternate route) and Road No. 6530 (mile 10.5).

6.6   Begin steep downhill section.

6.8   Bottom of steep section. Slightly downhill from this point.

7.9   Spur No. 800 and Minnehaha trailhead is 0.1 mile to the left. This is also the other end of the Hamaker Loop Trail. The signs for Lake West and Boundary Springs Trail have errors in distances.

        Cross the Rogue River on a bridge and start climbing uphill for a short distance to a level section.

8.3   Junction with spur No. 900 on left. Hamaker Campground is 0.5 miles south. The road is flat through this section and may have limited snow cover.

8.5   Junction with spur No. 950 on the left.

8.8   Junction with Highway 230. The mileage on the signs
        to Hamaker Campground and Lake West are in error.
        There is limited parking at this point, unless the
        snow cover is sparse. You are 12 miles north of the
        junction with Highway 62 and 13 miles from Union
        Creek Resort.

E8. HAMAKER LOOP

Trail Difficulty: Intermediate to advanced on road

Starting Point: USFS road No. 6530, 0.9 mile east
of Highway 230 (mile 7.9 on Lake
West trail); elevation 4050'

Trail Length: 10.6 miles (17.0 km) in a partial loop
[12.3 miles (19.8 km) in a commplete loop]

Elevation Change: Gain of 1600' at approximate half-way
point near Hamaker Bluff

Maps: USGS: Garwood Butte (15 min.)
USFS: Rogue River National Forest;
Trail guide from Prospect Ranger
District

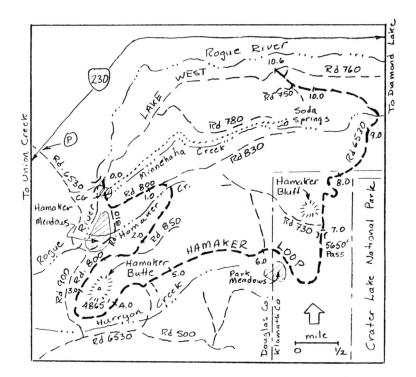

This trail is primarily used by snowmobilers, but is occasionally used by cross-country skiers. It requires a fairly substantial climb from either end, approaching a 10% grade in places. The trail winds around Hamaker Butte and Hamaker Bluff, following part of the old Minnehaha-Hurryon hiking trail. It also accesses Soda Springs and the new Minnehaha summer trail. Several good views are provided to the west and of Mt. Bailey to the north. An easier trip would be to ski in on the west section and into Soda Springs, a 2.9 mile one way trip, requiring only a moderate 350' climb. The main trail has an occasional orange diamond for guidance. The description follows the trail in a counterclockwise direction.

Mile	Description
0.0	Depending upon the snow conditions, you may have to park either on Highway 230, 0.9 miles to the west, or drive in on Road No. 6530, and cross the Rogue River bridge to the junction with spur No. 800.
	Spur No. 800 goes to the right parallel to the east bank of the Rogue River. The trail starts off on a level grade.
0.1	Minnehaha summer trail No. 1039 on the left (it is 3.0 miles to Soda Springs along this trail). Cross Minnehaha Creek and enter a campground.
0.4	Spur road No. 810 on right. Turn left and continue on spur No. 800 on a slight uphill grade.
1.2	Spur No. 830 on the left. This spur leads to Soda Springs 1.7 miles to the east. This is an enjoyable sidetrip involving only a 200' climb.
1.3	Switchback to the right and cross Hamaker Creek. Start uphill.
1.8	Large clear area from a burn on the right, providing a view to the west over Hamaker Meadows.
2.3	Spur No. 850 on left - turn right. Hamaker Butte is just to the south at 4865'.
2.7	Ski around Hamaker Butte and start uphill, heading south and then east above Hurryon Creek.
3.8	Begin a nearly level stretch.
4.6	Intersection with Road No. 6530 and end of spur No.

800. Straight ahead the road leads down to Highway 230 along National Creek, six miles to the south. Turn left and start a long uphill climb. (Note: this junction and turn is marked with orange diamonds and black arrows).

4.7   Spur No. 610 on right.

6.0   Large clear cut from a burn on the right.

6.1   Spur on left - Douglas/Klamath County line.

7.0   Top of climb - you are now at the high point on the trail. The trail is slightly downhill from here.

7.4   Start steeply downhill behind Hamaker Bluff.

7.6   Turn left and then right through a series of switch-backs. The backside of Mt. Bailey is to the north.

8.0   Large clear cut on the right. The trail continues through several downhill and level sections. There are occasional views to the west.

9.6   Cross Minnehaha Creek and start uphill.

9.8   Start downhill again.

10.3   Junction with spur No. 750 on the left.

10.5   Junction with Lake West Trail coming out through the woods (mile 6.1).

10.6   Intersection with spur No. 760 on the right (the Lake West Trail at mile 6.2) - the alternate route.

From here it is 1.7 miles west back to your starting point, and 2.6 miles to Highway 230.

F. SKY LAKES WILDERNESS

Sky Lakes is one of the newest wilderness areas in Oregon, straddling the Southern Oregon Cascades from Crater Lake National Park to Lake of the Woods. It is approximately six miles wide and twenty seven miles long, ranging in elevation from 3800' to 9495'. The more than 400 lakes and ponds in the wilderness, were formed by either lava flows or glacial scour.

The landforms are the results of volcanic eruptions and subsequent glaciation. The two high points in the area, Mt. McLoughlin and Devils Peak, are remnants of old volcanoes, exhibiting the blocky texture of basalt or platy texture of andesite lavas. Recent volcanic eruptions are characteristic of the pumice soils from Mt. Mazama (now Crater Lake) and cinder cones such as Goose Nest and Goose Egg. Glaciers covered much of the area and sculpted "U"-shaped valleys such as Red Blanket and Cherry Creek. Glacial striations or scratches are visible above Margurette Lake and below Gardner Peak.

Of historical interest, the Squaw Lake Trail (Twin Ponds Trail) follows the route of the old Rancheria Trail, an Indian trail. In 1863, it was widened as a military wagon road between Jacksonville and Fort Klamath. A sign, marking its location is on the southwest shore of Fourmile Lake.

Winter access to Sky Lakes is difficult, as most trailheads are at least five miles from the nearest plowed road. The most common access is from State Highway 140 between Lake of the Woods and Fish Lake. The Lower Canal and Pacific Crest are the most popular trails. Other access points are from the West Side road along Upper Klamath Lake or from Butte Falls on the west side. There are numerous Forest Service logging roads leading into the area - a few are described in the proceeding sections.

Two main trails traverse the wilderness area from north to south: the Pacific Crest Trail and the old Skyline Trail. Most of these trails are poorly marked and difficult to follow in the winter. Some have double blazes, and junctions are marked with carved wooden signs for summer use, however within wilderness areas it is not marked for Nordic skiing. Recent Region 6 Forest Service policy is to remove all trail signs in wilderness areas, except at trailheads and trail junctions.

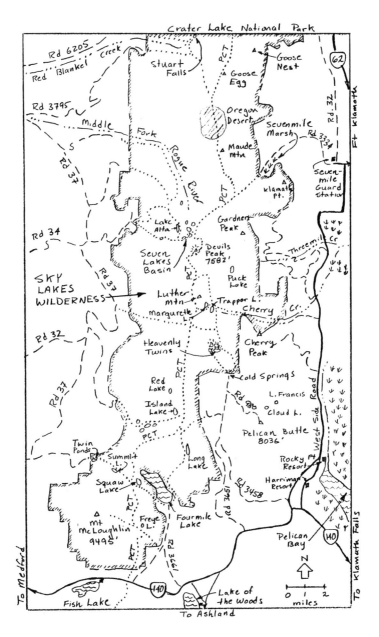

Crater Lake National Park

Rd 6205
Red Blanket Creek
Stuart Falls
PCT
Goose Nest
62
Rd 3795
Middle Fork Rogue River
Goose Egg
Oregon Desert
Sevenmile Marsh
Rd 33
Rd 32
S
Rd 37
Maude Mtn
Klamath Pt.
PCT
Sevenmile Guard Station
Rd 34
Lake Alta
Gardner Peak
Seven Lakes Basin
Devils Peak 7582'
Puck Lake
Threemile Cr.
SKY LAKES WILDERNESS
Rd 37
Luther Mtn
Marguerite
Trapper L.
Cherry Cr.
Rd 32
Rd 37
Heavenly Twins
PCT
Cherry Peak
Red Lake
Cold Springs
L. Francis
Island Lake
Rd 980
Cloud L.
PCT
Pelican Butte 8036'
Twin Ponds
Summit L.
Long Lake
Rocky Pt Resort
Squaw Lake
Rd 3458
Rd 3451
Harriman Resort
West Side Road
Freye O.L.
Fourmile Lake
Mt McLoughlin 9495'
PCT
Rd 3661
Pelican Bay
140
To Medford
PCT
N
To Klamath Falls
Fish Lake
140
Lake of the Woods
0 1 2 miles
To Ashland

Ft Klamath

F1.   SEVEN LAKES BASIN

Trail Difficulty: Advanced on road and trail

Starting Point: East side approach:
                           Four miles west of Fort Klamath on
                           county road 1419 at USFS Sevenmile
                           Guard Station; elevation 4200'

                           An alternate route from the
                           Medford area, is to enter from
                           the west along USFS road No. 3780
                           (described at the end of the east
                           side approach)

Trail Length: 10.3 miles (16.6 km) to Middle
                           Lake in Seven Lakes Basin, one way

Elevation Change: 1000' to Middle Lake

Maps: USGS: Pelican Butte (15 min.);
                                  Rustler Peak (15 min.)
                           USFS: Winema National Forest; Rogue
                                  River National Forest; The
                                  Sky Lakes Area;   Pacific
                                  Crest National Scenic Trail -
                                  Oregon Central Portion

The   Seven   Lakes Basin is a beautiful glacial basin   with   six
large   and   numerous   smaller   lakes, dominated by   Devil's   Peak
(elevation 7582) to the south.   These lakes feed   into the Middle
Fork of the Rogue River, a classic glacial U-shaped valley.

The access to   the   basin   is   by a logging and recreation road
from Sevenmile Guard Station   to   Sevenmile   Marsh   over   a   long
climb.   I have violated my   purist   cross country skiing code and
ridden   a   snowmobile   to   this   point   (my   only   time   on   a
snowmobile!).   Beyond Sevenmile Marsh is the Sky Lakes Wilderness
area, and part of the trail   follows   the   Pacific   Crest   summer
trail.

The trail is not marked for winter travel,   so   rely   on blazes
and the silver-gray Pacific   Crest Trail diamonds.   The diamonds
may be removed according recent USFS policy.

An alternate approach is   from   the   west   side   through   Butte
Falls, USFS highway 34, logging road No.   3780,   and   the   Seven
Lakes Trail   past   Frog Lake. This trail will be described at the
end of the east side section.

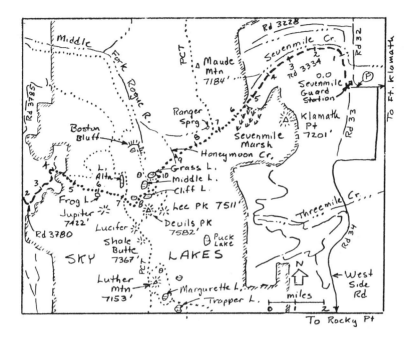

Mile	Description
0.0	Park near the Sevenmile Guard Station or on USFS Road No. 3334, depending upon the snow level. In early fall or late spring, you may be able to drive much of the way to Sevenmile Marsh.

Do not turn right from the guard station, but ski west on Road No. 3334 crossing Sevenmile Creek. |
0.3	Road No. 3334 turns right and heads due north, on a level grade parallel to the west bank of Sevenmile Creek.
1.5	The road turns left (west) and starts to climb, staying to the south of Sevenmile Creek. The grade averages 6% from here to Sevenmile Marsh.
5.6	Sevenmile Marsh and campground - end of the road.

Start climbing the trail marked with blazes. It initially crosses Sevenmile Creek on a wooden bridge and enters the Sky Lakes Wilderness.

7.4   Intersection with the Pacific Crest Trail indicated by a carved wood sign. The trail is now marked with silver-gray diamonds. Remember these are at summer-time heights; thus they may be near the snow line in winter.

The trail continues to climb another 400 feet; however, there are level areas and even downhill stretches.

9.1   Cross Honeymoon Creek.

9.8   Grass Lake can be seen through the trees below the trail. The marsh at the end of this lake is an old snow depth measurement course used by the Soil Conservation Service. The end marking post may still be seen.

10.0   Intersection with trail to Middle Lake. This trail goes right and descends about 100' to the lake.

10.3   East shore of Middle Lake.

*   *   *   *   *   *   *   *   *

10.4   Staying on the Pacific Crest Trail and climbing another 50 feet, you intersect the trail to Cliff Lake and to the west side of the Sky Lakes Wilderness. It is 0.5 mile to Cliff Lake.

You can continue up the trail to Devil's Peak, however this would be very difficult in the winter due to the steepness of the trail and drifting snow. The peak is almost 1400 feet above this junction.

12.3   Pass and top of climb - junction with Devils Peak trail. This trail is hard to identify, but follows the ridge to the right.

12.8   Summit of Devils Peak.

*   *   *   *   *   *   *   *   *

West Side Access

The access from the west side is through Butte Falls. Drive east out of Butte Falls on USFS Highway 34 sixteen miles to South

Fork Camp at elevation 4000'. Depending upon the snow level, proceed east on USFS Highway 37 0.4 mile to Road No. 3780. It may be necessary to ski from this point (elevation 4080')

Mile	Description

0.0   Ski east and uphill on Road No. 3780. The trail switchbacks left and then right.

1.2   Junction with spur road No. 200 - keep right. Ski south switchback to the northeast in 1.0 mile.

3.0   Another switchback to the left and one to the right along the Sky Lakes Wilderness boundary.

4.0   Trailhead for the Seven Lakes Trail and the King Spruce Trail, No. 981 and 980, respectively. Elevation 5300', where there is a well developed summer parking area.

Ski east along a ridge line, climbing at 13%.

4.5   Junction of Trails No. 981 and 980. Take the right branch to Frog Lake.

6.0   Frog Lake on the right. Continue climbing.

7.0   Intersection with Devil's Peak Trail on the right. It is a 1.0-mile climb to the Pacific Crest Trail and 1.5 miles to the top of Devil's Peak (elevation 7582').

7.2   Intersection with Lake Alta trail on the left, at 7000'. It is 0.3 mile north to the south end of Lake Alta. You are now at a saddle providing a view of Devil's Peak, some of the lakes below to the northeast, and the Crater Lake Rim. Start downhill.

8.2   South Lake on the left. Continue downhill.

8.5   Cliff Lake on the right. The trail is level for a short stretch.

8.6   Trail to Middle Lake goes downhill to the left.

9.0   Intersection with the Pacific Crest Trail - the same point as mile 10.4 on the east side access description.

F2. CHERRY CREEK

Trail Difficulty:	Intermediate on road and trail
Starting Point:	West side road of Upper Klamath Lake, 10 miles north of junction with Highway 140; elevation 4265'
Trail Length:	4.7 miles (7.6 km) to back of glacial valley, one way
Elevation Change:	Gain of 635'
Maps:	USGS: Pelican Butte (15 min.) USFS: Winema National Forest; The Sky Lakes Area

Cherry Creek runs through a beautiful U-shaped glacial valley, one of the few south of Crater Lake National Park in Klamath County. The trail follows the creek, crosses it several times on a logging road and trail. The road portion is the easiest to follow, the trail on the upper end presenting more of a challenge. The trail is best skied when the weather is colder and after a recent snowfall at the Upper Klamath Lake level. At this low elevation, snow condition are not always favorable.

Mile	Description
0.0	No parking is available at the trailhead; thus you must park along the shoulder of the county road. The trail, Road No. 3450, is marked with a large sign.
	Start skiing uphill.
0.1	Road junction, take the leg to the right. The trail climbs steadily from here.
1.2	The trail switchbacks under a small hill and climbs to the left. At the top, a spur road leads right into a quarry - an area to practice downhill running. At the bottom, the spur road leads back to the main trail at the base of the switch-back hill.
	The trail is level beyond this point.
1.5	Spur road turns left. Keep right and straight ahead.
1.8	Road ends and the Cherry Creek summer trail begins. The boundary of the Sky Lakes Wilderness is just ahead.

Ski downhill, winding through the trees. Watch for the summer blazes on trees - no other trail markings are used.

2.0   The trail levels out and follows the south bank of Cherry Creek. It is easy to get lost crossing some of the small meadows. Look for the blazes and keep Cherry Creek on your right.

3.5   The trail turns right and crosses Cherry Creek on a wood bridge - a good lunch stop. Cherry Peak, 1800 feet above you, is due south.

Cross the creek and continue along the north side. The trail is still fairly level. You are at the bottom of the U-shaped glacial valley.

4.7   A major crossing of Cherry Creek. There is no bridge and this is the end of the glacial valley. Suggest turning back over your same route.

If you are able to cross the creek, the trail then begins to climb steeply (at 20%) to Sky Lakes. Trapper or Horseshoe Lake is 1.3 miles away and 1000 feet higher. It is easy to get lost in this portion of the trail. I had difficulty in the spring, hiking across random snow patches - it is not well marked.

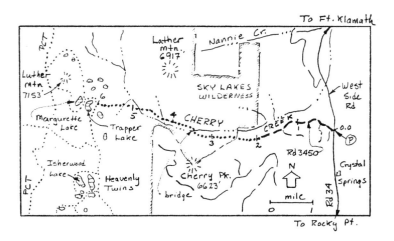

F3.   PACIFIC CREST

Trail Difficulty: Intermediate to advanced on trail

Starting Point: Sno-Park area on Highway 140, 0.6 mile
                       west of summit; 2.0 miles east of Fish
                       Lake Road;   elevation 5050'

Length: 7.5 miles (12.1 km) from parking area
                       to Squaw Lake Trail

Elevation Change: Gain of 1210' at mile 4.2, then loss of
                       410' to Squaw Lake Trail

Maps: USGS: Mt. McLoughlin (15 min.)
                       USFS: Winema NF; Jackson Klamath Winter
                              Trails; The Sky Lakes Area

This trail can be long and difficult, requiring at least a
16-mile (26-km) round trip; however it can be skied in short
sections.   It can be used for a loop trip in conjuction with the
South Rye Trail, the McLoughlin Trail, the Lower Canal Trail and
the Squaw Lake Trail. It follows a winding course through heavily
wooded terrain along the east   flank of Mt. McLoughlin. The most
difficult and hardest to find section is north of the McLoughlin
Trail intersection, as this portion is little used in the
winter.   Almost all of the trail lies within the Sky Lakes
Wilderness area.

• My   two   favorite   loop   trips both start at the Highway 140
Sno-Park. The loops can be skied in either direction; however I
prefer to ski up the Lower Canal Trail and come back downhill on
the Pacific Crest Trail. The return trip is enjoyable, requiring
the use of step turns, but none very difficult or steep.   The
first loop, 1.8 miles (2.9 km) long, goes up the Lower Canal
Trail 0.5 mile, then left on the South Rye Trail extension for
0.4 mile, back along the Pacific Crest Trail 0.6 mile, and then
along the connecting trail and through the parking lot 0.3 mile
to the point of beginning. The second loop, 6.5 miles (10.5 km)
long, again goes up the Lower Canal Trail 2.1 mile to the Mt.
McLoughlin Trail head, then left on the Mt. McLoughlin Trail 1.0
mile (climbing a very steep section), back along the Pacific
Crest Trail 3.1 miles, and then along the connecting trail and
through the parking lot 0.3 mile to the start.

The Pacific Crest Trail has been marked with a mixture of
silver-gray diamonds, dark blue diamonds and a few dark blue
diamonds with green čenters. Double blazes are found on some
trees.   There are no trail markings beyond the McLoughlin Trail

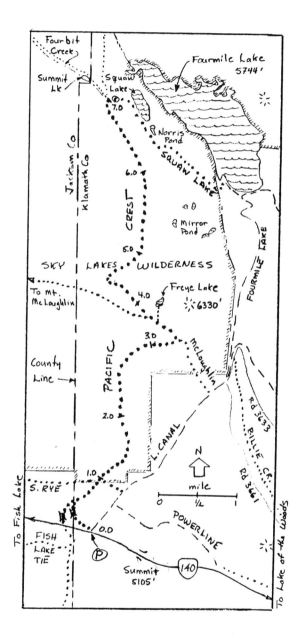

Fourbit Creek

Summit Lk

Squaw Lake
7.0

Fourmile Lake 5744'

Norris Pond

SQUAW LAKE

Jackson Co

Klamath Co

CREST 6.0

Mirror Pond

5.0

SKY LAKES WILDERNESS

To Mt. McLoughlin

4.0

Freye Lake
6330'

FOURMILE LAKE

3.0

McLoughlin

County Line

PACIFIC

2.0

Rd 3633

BILLIE CR.

L. CANAL

N

mile
0   ½

1.0

S. RYE

Rd 3661

To Fish Lake

FISH LAKE TIE

0.0

P

Summit 5105'

POWERLINE

140

To Lake of the Woods

123

intersection, except for a few the last 1.5 mile before the intersection with the Squaw Lake Trail. The Forest Service is presently removing all of the trail markings in wilderness areas, except at trailheads and trail junctions.

Mile	Description
0.0	Start in the Sno-Park area for the Lower Canal Trail (Rd. 3650) and ski left parallel to State Highway 140. This road leads into a large area, a parking lot and horse loading area in the summer. On the west side of this open area an access trail (No. 1000) starts through the woods, across a small bridge and meets the Pacific Crest Trail. The intersection is marked with engraved hiking signs.
0.3	The trail proceeds north from this intersection.
	You can also ski south along the Pacific Crest Trail here, a distance of 0.3 miles to State Highway 140. This portion of the trail is poorly marked and difficult to find; however it may be signed for this next season. It runs just east of a large lava flow, crosses a small bridge over the Cascade Canal, crosses the powerline and then Highway 140 just west (0.2 mile) of the Jackson-Klamath Co. line. Across the highway the trail connects with the Fish Lake Tie Trail.
	To the north, the trail climbs gradually through a series of turns.
0.9	Intersection with the South Rye Trail. The right leg goes to the Lower Canal Trail 0.4 miles away, and the left leg goes back down to Highway 140 3.6 miles away. Both are clearly marked with the standard blue diamonds on trees.
	Proceed across a small level plateau and then climb again through a series of curves.
3.4	Intersection with the Mt. McLoughlin Trail. It drops sharply to the right and leads to the Lower Canal Trail 1.0 miles to the southeast. Several engraved signs are on trees at this point, two with different spelling of McLoughlin. It is marked with a mixture of galvanized octogons,

dark blue diamonds and blazes.

The trail turns to the northwest at this point, climbing steeply. It is no longer marked for either summer or winter travel.

3.8 Intersection with the Freye Lake Trail on the right. This side trail, marked only with a small engraved hiking sign, is difficult to identify. The trail starts in a level area, goes over a small ridge and drops down to the lake, 0.3 mile away.

4.1 The Mt. McLoughlin summer trail goes off to the left. It is also difficult to identify; the engraved signs are placed high on the trees. Keep to the right.

4.2 Highest point on the trail at elevation 6260'. The trail drops off sharply to the northeast and traverses around a bowl along a sidehill.

5.0 The trail becomes less steep, proceeding almost due north.

6.0 A few dark blue diamonds with orange centers and the silver-gray Pacific Crest Trail diamonds can now be found.

7.2 The trail drops steeply with a small pond below and on your right.

7.5 Intersection with Squaw Lake Trail at the northwest end of a small pond. The trail to the right goes directly through the pond and is well marked for skiers. This is actually the summer Twin Pond Trail No. 993. The Fourmile Lake Trail and Fourmile Lake campground is 2.5 miles to the southeast. To the west is a small pond (0.1 mile), the Cascade Crest at elevation 5850' (0.2 mile), then downhill to Summit Lake (0.5 mile), and the Twin Pond Road No. 3760, is four miles away. It is 5.5 miles ahead along the Pacific Crest Trail to Island Lake.

F4. SQUAW LAKE

Trail Difficulty:	Intermediate on trail
Starting Point:	Fourmile Lake campground; elevation 5750'
Trail Length:	2.5 miles (4.0 km), one way
Elevation Change:	Gain of 100' to intersection with Pacific Crest Trail
Maps:	USGS: Mt. McLoughlin (15 min.) USFS: Winema National Forest; Jackson Klamath Winter Trails

This is probably one of the more difficulty trail to start as it requires a trip of at least 4.9 miles (7.9 km) from the nearest Sno-Park (via: Lower Canal and Fourmile Lake Trails). The trail follows the southwest shore of Fourmile Lake and ends at the Pacific Crest Trail. It is fairly flat with only one small climb, and skirts several small ponds and the larger Squaw Lake. The trail is in heavy timber and is marked with the standard blue diamonds with an occassional one dark blue with orange center.

Mile	Description
0.0	Start at the end of the Fourmile Lake Trail at the campgound at the south end of Fourmile Lake. Ski left (northwest) following the road along the shore.
0.2	Trailhead parking sign; the summer starting point for the trail. Do not take this turn as it is not marked for skiers.
0.3	Enter the turnaround for a campground. The trailhead is to the left - marked as "Twin Ponds Trail". A small piece of railroad track mounted on a pole marks the crossing of the "Route of Old Military Road, 1883-1909, Ft. Klamath to Jacksonville".
	Ski southeast, away from the lake, on a marked trail The trail will then gradually turn northwest.
0.5	Enter the Sky Lakes Wilderness; sign on the left.
1.0	Small pond on the right, and just ahead another small pond on the left.

1.5	Norris Lake on the right.
1.9	Start of Squaw Lake on the right.
2.2	End of Squaw Lake. The trail splits and starts uphill. The marked ski trail is the right branch, the summer hiking trail the left branch.
2.3	Top of hill, trails come back together.
2.4	Cross a small pond, the summer trail goes around to the right.
2.5	Intersection with the Pacific Crest Trail. This point is well marked with summer trail signs and winter ski signs.

Straight ahead the Twin Ponds Trail continues: 0.1 mile to the right side of small pond; 0.2 mile to the Cascade Summit (elevation 5850'), marked with a sign; then downhill 0.5 mile to Summit Lake; 3.0 miles to Twin Ponds; and finally 4.0 miles to the Twin Pond Road, No. 3760 (elevation 4800'). This trail is marked with double blazes on trees.

On the Pacific Crest Trail; Island Lake is 5.5 miles north, Freye Lake and Highway 140 are 4.0 and 8.0 miles south, respectively. See the Pacific Crest Trail log for a description of the trail south.

It is probably easiest to return over the same route, as the Pacific Crest Trail is difficult to follow and is not marked for winter travel.

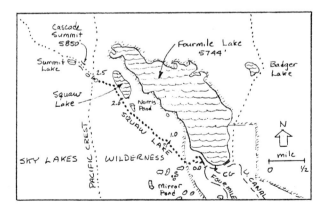

F5. PELICAN BUTTE

Trail Difficulty:	Advanced on road and off trail
Starting Point:	Highway 140 at junction of USFS Road No. 3651 (Cold Springs Road), 3.0 miles west of the junction with the Westside Road (0.5 mile east of bottom of Lake of the Woods grade); elevation 4200'
Trail Length:	12.5 miles (20.1 km) to the top of Pelican Butte; 3 to 4 miles (5 to 6.5 km) down to Westside Road
Elevation Change:	Gain of 3836'
Maps:	USGS: Pelican Butte (15 min.); Lake of the Woods (15 min.) USFS: Winema National Forest; The Sky Lakes Area; Jackson Klamath Winter Trails

Pelican Butte, a prominent shield volcano on the west side of Upper Klamath Lake, has long been used by cross country and downhill skiers. Local interests hope to develop it into a commercial winter recreation area. Its popularity is due to excellent snow condition throughout the winter and a variety of skiing terrain. The bowl (glacial cirque) on the northeast side is perferred by downhill skiers, and the remaining 25% slopes are used by cross country skiers.

Access to the 8036-foot summit can be gained by "timber bashing", however the usual route is by the primitive road up the west side. Many skiers prefer to ride a snowmobile or snowcat to the summit and then ski down east to the Westside Road. Snowmobile routes are along the Cold Springs Road (No. 3651) and the Old Pelican Butte Road (No. 3455 and 3458) for about nine miles (14.5 km), and then up the Pelican Butte primitive switchback road (spur No. 980), 3.5 miles (5.6 km) to the summit. A summer fire lookout is located here, and the view is spectacular.

From the summit you can ski the bowl northeast down to the Cloud Lake Group and Lake Francis, and then down to several spur roads (No. 230, 300, 305 and 302). An alternative route is to ski either east or southeast to Road No. 3456 or spur No. 230. These roads then connect down to the Westside Road near the Rocky Point area and Harriman and Rocky Point Lodges. All of these runs have many open areas, and some dense brush on the lower slopes. A telemark, mountain or convertable downhill binding is a must for these runs. You can't get lost as long as you head downhill, you just may not know exactly where you are on the mountain.

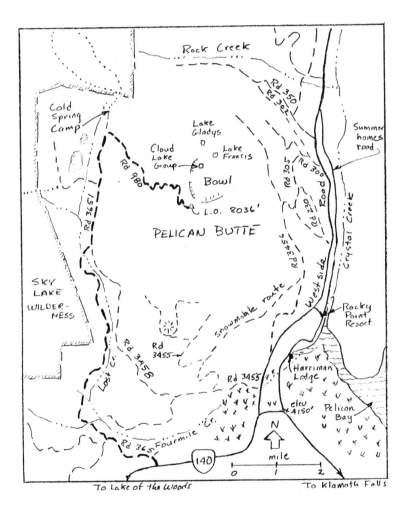

G. FREMONT - LAKEVIEW

Two cross country trail systems have recently been designated and marked by the Fremont National Forest in the Quartz Mountain and Warner Canyon areas. A third unmarked trail system is in the Gearhart Mountain Wilderness. These trails are east of Klamath Falls and the Rogue Valley. They offer beautiful country, a high percentage of good weather - typical of the high desert, and generally excellent snow.

Quartz Mountain pass is 13 miles east of Bly on State Highway 140 at 5500'. Both snowmobile and cross country trails head north and south from the pass. Fortunately there is very little overlap between the two uses. Gearhart Mountain Wilderness is about 15 miles northeast of Bly on Forest Service cooperative logging roads. Access to the trailheads depends upon winter plowing. Log haul in the winter is common in this area, so chances are good that some will be open. Check with the Bly Ranger District for local information.

Warner Canyon is about 10 miles east of Lakeview on State Highway 140. Several trails head north and south from the highway in the vicinity of the winter sports area. Some of these trails may not be marked for cross country skiing until the winter of 1988/89; however all follow Forest Service roads. These trails are over 5000' in elevation, with some climbing to 6500'. The winter sports area also has a tow for downhill skiing. Check with the Lakeview Ranger District for additional information.

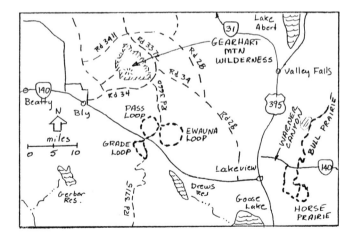

Trail Difficulty:	Advanced on trail
Starting Point:	Corral Creek campground on USFS Road No. 34, 15.5 miles northeast of Bly; elevation 5960'
Trail Length:	5.5 miles (8.9 km) to Gearhart Mountain saddle, one way
Elevation Change:	Gain of 2000' to saddle
Maps:	USGS: Fishhole Mtn. (15 min.); Sandhill Crossing (7.5 min.); Lee Thomas Crossing (7.5 min.)
	USFS: Fremont National Forest; The Gearhart Mountain Wilderness

Gearhart Mountain is a prominent volcanic dome easily seen from Highway 140 near Bly. From the top of the 8354-foot mountain the Steens Mountain to the east and the Cascade Peaks from Mt. Lassen to Three Sisters are visible on a clear day. Blue Lake, the only lake in the wilderness, is near the north boundary.

Three main trails access the wilderness: (1) Corral Creek in the southeast corner, (2) Nottin Creek in the north, and (3) Boulder Springs in the southwest corner. Access in the winter depends upon main roads being plowed for timber operations. If these access roads are not open, the ski trip would be much too long to be enjoyable. Road access is provided from Bly by USFS Road No. 34, connecting with either 018 and 3411 on the west side, or 3372 on the east side. An alternate access route is to ski from Road No. 3372 up Dairy Creek to the base of Gearhart Mountain. In fact, this may be the easiest route in the winter since a creek guides you.

The route from Corral Creek will be described, as this is the most accessible trailhead in the winter. Drive east from Bly on Highway 140 about one mile and then turn north for one-half mile and then east on USFS Road No. 34, the Campbell Reservoir road. Follow this road northeast for 14 miles to Corral Creek Campground. Hopefully, there will be a place to park.

Mile	Description
0.0	Corral Creek campground access road at junction with Road No. 34. Highway 3660 goes southeast. Ski west on the campground road.

131

0.2   Corral Creek campground. Continue on the road
                to the west through several switchbacks.

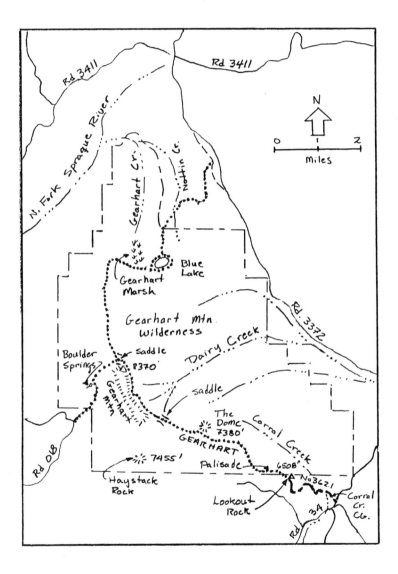

1.7   Lookout Rock and summer trail head; elevation 6400'. Start following Trail No. 100 just south of Lookout Rock, heading northwest.

2.1   Wilderness boundary and the Palisade Rocks. These vertical columns and mounds of volcanic rock are an interesting example of nature's erosional power. The trail will be difficult to follow through these formations - head northwest along the upper edge of the open area.

                The trail begins climbing, approaching 10% in about a mile. Go through a switchback just before The Dome.

3.8   The Dome - a large weathered volcanic monolith that rises several hundred feet above the trail.

                Ski along the south side of The Dome and start heading due west and then southwest around a ridge.

4.3   View to the south - Haystack Rock is a little less than a mile to the southwest. Swing around a large switchback and head northwest, climbing steeply.

5.5   Saddle just to the east of the main Gearhart Mountain ridge. A great view to the south. The head waters of Dairy Creek can been seen below in the valley to the north.

                You can follow the trail down into the Dairy Creek Valley and climb the ridge to the northwest where the trail continues down to Blue Lake. You can also climb Gearhart Mountain from here. It is 300' to 400' above this saddle.

                It is 4.5 miles out to Road No. 3372 if you follow the Dairy Creek Valley to the east, or 5.0 miles to Blue Lake. I would recommend heading back over your original route.

G2. EWAUNA LOOP

Trail Difficulty:	Intermediate on road
Starting Point:	USFS Road No. 3660, 1.6 miles northwest of Highway 140 on Quartz Mountain Pass; elevation 5560'
Trail Length:	6.5 miles (10.5 km) in a loop
Elevation Change:	Loss of 200' to approximate half-way point.
Maps:	USGS: Fishhole Mtn. (15 min.) USFS: Fremont National Forest; Orientation Map - Quartz Pass Winter Sports Area

The description of this trail is approximate only; the actual trail should be marked on the ground (courtesy of USFS - Bly District) by the winter of 1987/88. The trail will circle 6279-foot high Quartz Butte, site of recent gold mining exploration, and follow primitive spur roads. The trail will be marked with the standard blue diamonds.

Depending upon mining activity in the winter, Road No. 3660 may be plowed the 1.6 miles to Ewauna Camp meadow. If the road is not open, you will have to ski from Quartz Mountain Pass on a single lane (paved) road, climbing about 100', or follow the east portion of the Pass Loop Trail. Road No. 3660 is also a snowmobile trail leading to the Quartz Loop Trail farther to the northeast. A Sno-Park is planned for the pass and some parking will probably be available at Ewauna Camp.

Mile	Description
0.0	Start at Ewauna Camp meadow, a large open area on the southeast side of the road. The description will start in the clockwise direction around Quartz Butte.
	Ski along the north side of the meadow parallel and just below Road No. 3660.
0.1	Enter the trees and start slightly uphill.
0.6	Pass wooden corrals and start downhill to the right into Angel Spring drainage.

1.5	Spur road on right.
2.1	Angel Camp and Angel Springs on the left. Ski along the west side of the drainage, still heading slightly downhill.
3.8	Enter Quartz Valley and pass under a power line. You are now at the low point on the trail. Start back uphill, following the power line.
4.6	Leave the power line and head northwest.
6.0	Spur road goes to the right and uphill to a mine. There should also be evidence of mining activity and equipment in the area. A large borrow pit is located to the west about 500'. The road to the left goes out to Road No. 3660, about 0.5 mile away. Continue straight ahead.

Ski along the east side of a meadow and back into the lower end of the Ewauna Camp meadow. |
| 6.5 | Intersection with Road No. 3660 and your starting point. |

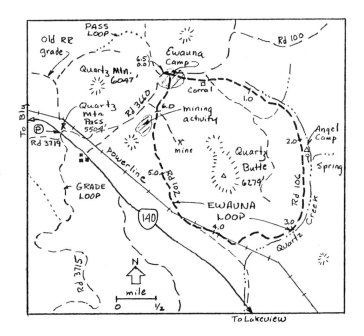

G3. PASS LOOP

Trail Difficulty: Intermediate on road and trail

Starting Point: Quartz Mountain Pass on Highway 140,
13 miles east of Bly; elevation 5504'

Trail Length: 4.2 miles (6.8 km) in a loop

Elevation Change: Gain of 300' to approximate half-way
point

Maps: USGS: Fishhole Mtn. (15 min.)
USFS: Fremont National Forest;
Orientation Map - Quartz Pass
Winter Sports Area

The description of this trail is approximate only; the actual trail should be marked on the ground (courtesy of USFS - Bly District) by the winter of 1987/88. The trail will circle 6047-high Quartz Mountain on an old railroad grade, primitive spur roads, a new trail and part of a paved road. The trail will be marked with the standard blue diamonds.

Depending upon mining activity in the winter, part of the trail on Road No. 3660 may be plowed the 1.6 miles to Ewauna Camp meadow. Road No. 3660 is also a snowmobile trail leading to the Quartz Loop Trail to the northeast. A Sno-Park is planned for the pass, the start of this trail.

Mile   Description

0.0   Start at Quartz Mountain Pass on the north side. The description will move in the clockwise direction around Quartz Mountain.

Ski up Road No. 3660 about 0.1 mile and turn left on the spur road just after the power line.

0.1   Ski under the power line and turn right after 0.1 mile on the old railroad grade. Continue nearly level on the railroad grade

0.5   Leave the railroad grade and turn right on a spur road. Start climbing steeply to the northeast.

1.0   You are now at a saddle where you will leave the spur road and follow a new trail.

Continue heading uphill and to the northeast.

1.5   The high point on the trail. Turn to the southeast
       and head downhill.

2.0   Turn right on a spur road and head steeply downhill.

2.6   Intersection with Road No. 3660 at Ewauna Camp meadow.
       This is the start of the Ewauna Loop Trail to the east.

       Turn southwest and head downhill on a spur road parallel
       to the west side of Road No. 3660.

3.3   Leave the spur road and ski along the west side of Road
       No. 3660 - note that this is also a snowmobile trail.

4.2   Quartz Mountain Pass, your starting point.

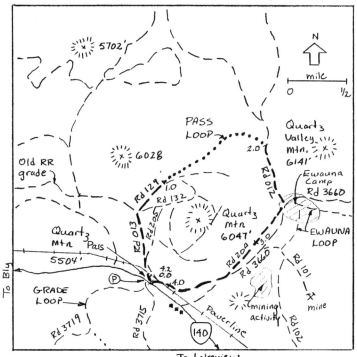

To Lakeview

G4. GRADE LOOP

Trail Difficulty:	Beginning to intermediate on road
Starting Point:	Quartz Mountain Pass on Highway 140, 13 miles east of Bly; elevation 5504'
Trail Length:	3.1 miles (5.0 km) in a loop
Elevation Change:	Gain of 220' at approximate half-way point
Maps:	USGS: Fishhole Mtn. (15 min.)
	USFS: Fremont National Forest; Orientation Map - Quartz Pass Winter Sports Area

The description of this trail is approximate only; the actual trail should be marked on the ground (courtesy of USFS - Bly District) by the winter of 1987/88. The trail will circle a small hill on an old railroad grade and spur roads, and will be marked with the standard blue diamonds. A Sno-Park is planned for the pass, the start of this trail. Road No. 3715, the old railroad grade, is also used by snowmobilers to gain access to the Fishhole Loop to the southwest.

Mile	Description
0.0	Start on the south side of Quartz Mountain Pass. The description will move clockwise around the hill.
	Ski up Road No. 3715 (paved), the old railroad grade. This is a steady climb to the south, with occasional views through the trees to the east of the mining activity on Quartz Butte. Watch for snowmobilers.
	About 100' south from the pass, Road No. 3719 comes in on the right - this is part of the return loop.
1.1	The trail turns right on a spur road.
	Ski uphill for a short distance (0.4 mile) through heavey timber and then start downhill along the east side of a small draw.
1.7	Intersection with a spur road on the left.
1.9	Start downhill.

2.4   Intersection with Road No. 3719 at a switchback across a draw. Turn right on this road and ski north on a fairly level grade. The trail then circles the hill and heads east.

3.0   Ski down a short hill, and intersect Road No. 3715 and Quartz Mountain Pass, your starting point.

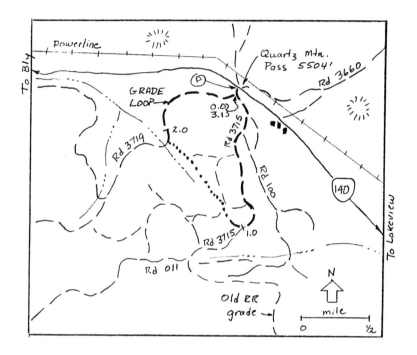

G5. WARNER CANYON

The Warner Canyon Winter Sport Area is located 7.0 miles east
of Lakeview on Highway 140. It has been noted as a downhill
skiing area, but there has been recently interest in developing a
cross country ski area. The Highlands Ski Club, in cooperation
with the Fremont National Forest has proposed three ski trails
starting from the ski area. These are trails (1) to the City of
Lakeview, (2) south to Camas Prairie, and (3) north to Bull
Prairie. The actual signing of these trails may not be completed
until the winter of 1988/89. Check with the Lakeview Ranger
District for details (address in the Appendix).

G6. BULL PRAIRIE

An unofficial trail runs north of Highway 140 to Squaw Butte
and Bull Prairie. Parking is available 4.0 miles east of the
Warner Canyon Winter Sports Area on Highway 140. Ski north on
USFS Road No. 3615. Squaw Butte is 4.0 miles north and Bull
Prairie is 6.0 miles north.

G7. HORSE PRAIRIE

An unofficial trail has been used south of Highway 140 to
Summit Prairie and Horse Prairie. Parking is available 4.0 miles
east of the Warner Canyon Winter Sports Area on Highway 140,
opposite the Bull Prairie road. Ski south on USFS Road No. 3910.
Summit Prarie is 2.0 miles south and Horse Prairie is 5.0 miles
south. Make a loop trip back by continuing on Road No. 3910 west
and then north on Road No. 3915 to Highway 140. From here it is
1.3 miles east back to your starting point. The loop trip is
15.0 miles (24.1 km).

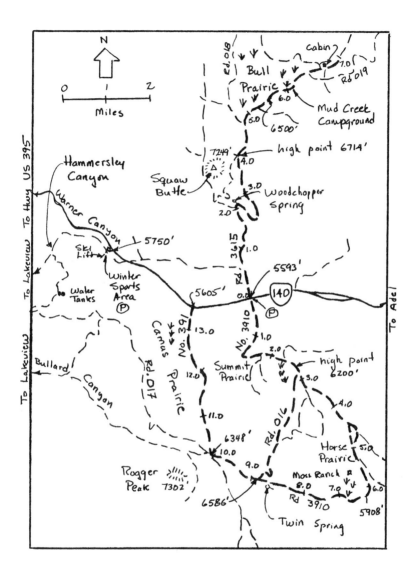

H. FISH LAKE - LAKE OF THE WOODS AREA

The Fish Lake - Lake Of The Woods area probably has more clear days in the winter than other ski areas in the state. Located halfway between Medford and Klamath Falls, it is traversed by State Highway 140. From this route over 50 miles of cross country ski trails are available, half of which have been marked in cooperation with the Forest Service and the Grants Pass Nordic Ski Club. The area is split between Jackson and Klamath Counties, and between the Rogue River and the Winema National Forests.

Resorts at both lakes provide food and lodging on weekends; however, their schedule can vary, thus check by calling the phone numbers listed in the Appendix if you are in doubt. A short distance to the west, a third resort, Rocky Point on Upper Klamath Lake, also offers food and lodging. I have always enjoyed skiing in this area and then finishing the day at one of the lodges in front of a warm fire sipping my favorite drink.

The summit on the highway between the two lakes is at elevation 5105 feet, Lake Of The Woods at 4949 feet and Fish Lake at 4679 feet. Trees shelter most of the trails which follow Forest Service roads or improved trails, and are of a beginning to intermediate difficulty. With many new trails added to the system in the last few years, short and intermediate loop trips are possible. All trails are marked with large blue diamonds placed eight to ten feet above the ground on trees. A free map from the Forest Service, "Jackson Klamath Winter Trails," traces cross country ski trails and snowmobile routes in the area. Few conflicts exist between ski and snowmobile traffic.

Two large volcanic mountains dominating the area provide backdrops for photographs, and some challenging climbs and downhill runs for the advanced skier. Mt. McLoughlin, visible from both Medford and Klamath Falls, is 9495-foot high. The larger of the two peaks, it is an unusual armour plated cinder cone with a large glacial cirque on the northeast side exposing the cindery core. Brown Mountain, six miles to the southeast, is 7311-foot high, a classic shield volcano of basaltic lava. The Pacific Crest Trail traverses the flanks of both.

You can reach the area in less than an hour by driving northeast from Medford or northwest from Klamath Falls on Highway 140. Parking is available near each lodge, or three locations along the north side of the highway. Other parking areas along the highway are used primarily by snowmobilers. All require an Oregon Sno-Park permit displayed on the dashboard of your car. These are available at both resorts.

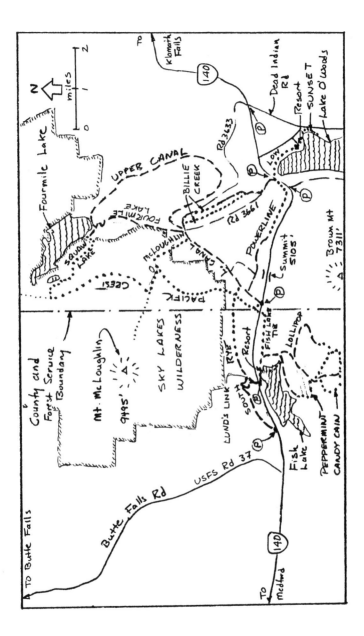

143

Trail Difficulty:	Beginning on trail
Starting Point:	Lake of the Woods Resort; elevation 4950'
Trail Length:	1.5 miles (2.4 km), one way
Elevation Change:	5 feet along lake shore
Maps:	USGS: Lake of the Woods (15 min.)
	USFS: Winema National Forest

The sunset trail follows a summer hiking trail that connects the Lake of the Woods Resort with the Sunset Campground area. The trail follows along the east side of the lake around Rainbow Bay. It is not well marked but the opening through the trees is fairly easy to follow, or you can just ski along the lake shore.

Mile	Description
0.0	Start from the parking lot at the Lake of the Woods dock area across from the ski/boat rental building. Parking is available here or at the resort area, 0.1 mile north.
	The starting point is marked with a blue sign and diamonds. Ski south through the woods parallel to the lake shore. The trail is between the lake and rest rooms, however you can follow the road just to the east of the rest rooms.
0.8	Rainbow Bay Campground and road turn-around. Look for the summer Sunset Trail sign or follow the wide opening through the woods.
1.0	The trail goes around a marsh area at Rainbow Bay, very close to Dead Indian Road. From here it turns back towards the lake and enters heavy timber.
1.2	The trail is now within 50 feet of the lake. You can either follow the trail or ski along the lake shore.
1.5	Intersect the boat launching site for Sunset Campground. This is the end of the trail as marked by another sign. You can continue around the lake or

return by the same route. An alternate is to ski
east and then return along the campground access
road back to the 1.0 mile point.

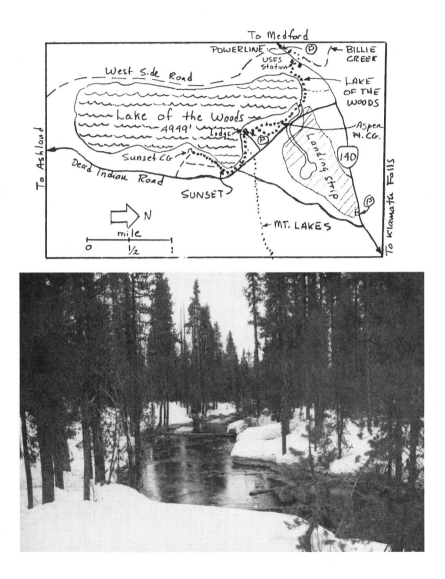

H2. LAKE OF THE WOODS

Trail Difficulty:	Beginning on road and trail
Starting Point:	Lake of the Wood Lodge; elevation 4960'
Trail Length:	1.5 miles (2.4 km) one way
Elevation Change:	25 feet
Maps:	USGS: Lake of the Woods (15 min.)
	USFS: Winema National Forest; Jackson Klamath Winter Trails

   This trail follows the northeast shore of Lake of the Woods, connecting the lodge area with the ranger station on Highway 140. By crossing the highway from the ranger station you can connect with Powerline and Billie Creek trails. To the south, you can continue on the Sunset Trail. The trail first follows a road through a wooded campground and then crosses a marsh area and Billie Creek before entering the ranger station compound. It is a pleasant trail with several nice gentle hills; however the trees can limit the snow cover, and warm weather make crossing the marsh and stream impossible. Although the trail is marked with the standard blue diamonds, they are sometimes difficult to find.

Mile	Description
0.0	Park at the Lake of the Woods resort and ski to the northeast of the lodge, restaurant and cabins. Turn north.
0.1	Intersection with the upper loop road of Aspen Point campground. The trail splits. Ski to the right to loop in a clockwise direction.
0.2	Start down a long gentle hill on the campground road.
0.5	Cross the entrance road to the campground - to the left is the summer boat launching area. Ski across the road and follow the loop on the other side.
	You can return on the loop road by turning to the left, skiing west and then south past a rest room. The trail climbs a short hill and connects

connects to the original trail at mile 0.1.

0.7   Turn to the west at the end of the loop road. Ski to the left of the rest room and behind the sign board. Follow along the shore of the lake on top of a dike.

0.9   The end of this part of the dike is breached by a small stream coming from the landing strip area to the east. If you ski straight ahead along the continuation of the dike you will intersect a snowmobile trail along the north side of the lake. If you cannot cross the the marsh and Billie Creek because the weather is warm, this route can be followed to the ranger station.

Turn left at the breach in the dike and ski across the marsh area along the north edge of the lake. You should see a blue diamond on a tree cross the marsh.

1.0   Cross the inlet of Billie Creek. You may have to go upstream to find a suitable crossing point.

1.3   Turn north into the woods towards the ranger station. There is a blue diamond at this point.

Do not continue south along the lake; however, when the lake is frozen, you can make a loop south along the shore and then back across the lake to the lodge.

1.4   Cross the snowmobile trail and enter the ranger station compound. Continue north between the buildings - there are no more blue diamonds.

1.5   Intersection with Highway 140. If you cross to the north side, you will intersect the Powerline trail about 0.1 mile west of the start of the Billie Creek Trail. There is parking along the highway 0.1 mile west on the south side, and 0.1 mile east on the north side.

See Sunset Trail for a detailed map.

H3. BILLIE CREEK LOOP

Trail Difficulty:	Intermediate on road and trail
Starting Point:	Sno-Park on Highway 140, 1.3 miles east of the summit and just east of the Lake of the Woods Ranger Station; elevation 5000'
Trail Length:	6.0 miles (9.6 km) in a loop
Elevation Change:	650' gain at half-way point
Maps:	USGS: Lake of the Woods (15 min.) USFS: Winema National Forest; Sky Lakes Area; Jackson Klamath Winter Trails

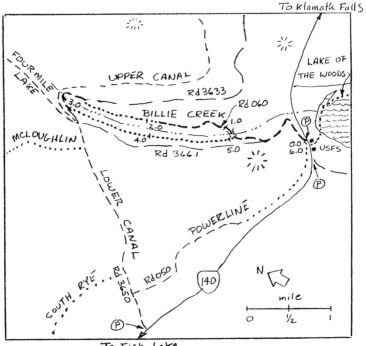

This trail loops around Billie Creek between Highway 140 and the Cascade Canal. The first part of the trail is shared with snowmobilers, but there is plenty of room to ski on the shoulders of the road. The trail can be used to connect to the Fourmile Lake and Upper Canal trails, or as part of another loop with Lower Canal and Powerline trails. This latter loop is 8.3 miles (13.4 km) long. Most of the trail is in the woods on either side of Billie Creek and has no difficult sections. All except the lower portion of the trail on Road No. 3661 is marked with the standard blue diamonds.

Mile	Description
0.0	Start at the Sno-Park on the north side of Highway 140, where there is room for about 10 cars. The Powerline Trail goes to the left along a snowmobile route. Ski uphill and to the northeast along the West Fourmile Lake snowmobile route (Road No. 3661).
0.6	Turn off to the right on spur No. 060 and ski downhill. This junction is marked with a cross country skier sign.
0.9	Billie Creek crossing. The trail splits to form the loop around the creek. The east branch continues on spur No. 060 across the creek. The west branch begins on a trail at the west edge of the bridge. I will describe the trail in a counterclockwise direction.
	Ski across the bridge and follow the road along the east side of Billie Creek.
2.0	End of the spur road - continue uphill along a trail.
2.7	The trail turns to the right and climbs on a moderately steep grade.
2.8	Intersection with Road No. 3633 - the West Fourmile Lake snowmobile route. Turn left and ski along the road. If you are skiing the loop in the opposite direction, the trail is difficult to locate - look for the blue diamond part-way down the slope.
2.9	Cross the headwaters of Billie Creek on the road and switchback to the left.
3.0	Intersection with the other branch of the trail. This is also the high point. The Cascade Canal and the Upper Canal Trail is just above the road - you can see the bank through the trees. The

intersection of roads 3650, 3661 and 3633 and the
Lower Canal and Fourmile Lake trails is 0.1 mile
west along the road. This intersection is also
difficult to find because the blue trail sign
is hidden beneath the branches of a tree and faces
east.

Turn left and ski downhill through an open area.
The trail then winds through the trees on a fairly
gentle grade. You are now skiing on the west bank
of Billie Creek.

5.1   Intersection with spur No. 060 at the Billie Creek
        bridge (mile 0.9). This completes the loop - return
        to the Sno-Park along first part of the trail.

6.0   Sno-Park on Highway 140.

H4. LOWER CANAL

Trail Difficulty:	Intermediate on road
Starting Point:	State Highway 140, 0.6 mile west of summit; 2.0 miles east of Fish Lake Rd; elev. 5050'
Trail Length:	2.4 miles to Jct with Fourmile Lake Road and Upper Canal Trail
Elevation Change:	Gain of 610 feet to junction
Maps:	USGS: Mt. McLoughlin (15 min.) and Lake of the Woods (15 min.)
	USFS: Winema NF; The Sky Lakes Area; and Jackson Klamath Winter Trails

This is one of my favorate ski trails allowing easy access to higher elevations for drier snow, providing access to a variety of other trails, and sloping downhill coming out. The trail has a variety of terrain, with moderate climbs spaced between flat sections. It is also a popular trail; thus odds are that you will find a broken track when you arrive.

The trail head and parking area are located on the north side of State Highway 140, with space for approximately 10 cars.

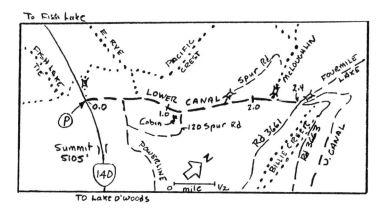

Mile	Description

0.0   Start by following the road uphill to the northeast. The road to the left (west) leads to the unplowed Pacific Crest Trailhead parking lot and to the Pacific Crest Trail described in another section.

0.1   Junction with a powerline. The trail climbs a short hill and then opens onto a large meadow to the east.

0.3   Road No. 050 (Powerline Trail) begins to the east. Start up the second major hill.

0.5   The South Rye Trail comes in from the west near the top of the second hill. It is marked with a blue arrow and diamond, but may be somewhat hard to see as trees hide it from view. The Cascade Canal from Four Milelake to Fish Lake parallels the trail on the west side.

1.0   A logging spur Road, No. 120, intersects from the east leading into an open logged area for half to three quarters of a mile, a pleasant side trip. You can continue along this spur road, descending for about half a mile to a connection with the Powerline Trail, providing a loop trip. Just south of this intersection is a small cabin in the trees to the east - the large rock mound to the west is the elevated Cascade Canal. The trail continues continues along a flat section and then up a third hill.

1.5   A logging spur road intersects from the west, providing a good view of Mt. McLoughlin. It crosses the Cascade Canal and then turns north. The upper end, approximately one mile away and 360 feet higher in elevation, is just short of the Mt. McLoughlin Trail. If you like to "timber bash," you may be able to locate the trail several hundred yards to the north.

From here the trail climbs through a narrow and steep section.

2.1   A small clearing for the Mt. McLoughlin Trailhead parking lot. The actual trail starts to the west, marked by a sign. A small wooden bridge is in the trees, crossing the Cascade Canal. A beautiful open meadow is on the other side.

This trailhead provides a short access to the Pacific Crest Trail, allowing a loop ski trip.

The connection is slightly less than a mile; however the elevation gain is about 350 feet and quite steep near the west end. It is probably easier to climb than to ski down. It is marked with a mixture of galvanized octogons, dark blue diamonds and blazes.

2.4 Junction with the Fourmile Lake Road (No. 3661), Billie Creek Road (No. 3633) and the Cascade Canal Road (No. 290). The latter is blocked by a gate. If the snow is not too deep you'll see a large four-sided sign in the middle of the intersection. From this point it is:

> 2.6 miles (4.2 km) to Fourmile Lake via Road
> No. 3661 (Fourmile Lake Trail)
> 6.5 miles (10.5 km) to Fourmile Lake via
> Cascade Canal Road (Upper Canal Trail)
> 3.0 miles (4.8 km) to Hwy 140 along the Billie
> Creek Trail parallel to Rd. No. 3661.

All of these trails are described in other sections.

H5. UPPER CANAL

Trial Difficulty:	Beginning on canal bank road
Starting Point:	Intersection of roads 3650, 3661, and 3633. Mile 2.4 on Lower Canal Trail; elevation 5660'
Trail Length:	6.5 miles (10.5 km) to Fourmile Lake; 9.1 miles 14.6 km) round trip by Road No. 3661 (Fourmile Lake Trail)
Elevation Change :	Gain of 84 feet to Fourmile Lake
Maps:	USGS: Lake of the Woods (15 min.) USFS: Winema NF; The Sky Lakes Area; Jackson Klamath Winter Trails

Access this trail from State Highway 140 to the south by either the Lower Canal Trail (2.4 miles) or by the Billie Creek Trail (3.0 miles), the former providing the easiest access.

The Upper Canal Trail follows the maintenance road on the bank of the Cascade Canal running from Fourmile Lake to Fish Lake. It is one of the easiest trails to ski in this area because of its nearly flat grade. The road is surrounded by trees as it circles the 6434-foot high Rye Spur. It has the advantage of being reserved for cross country skiing use; however the lack of scenic view and varied terrain can make the entire trip someone boring.

Mile	Description
0.0	Start by going around the barrier on the northeast side of the intersection keeping the canal ditch on your left. The road goes northeast for about 0.2 miles, paralleling East Billie Creek Road, below and to the south. The road then heads southeast.
2.4	Cross the Rye Spur summer hiking trail (the old Pacific Crest Trail). At this point the road turns northeast and eventually northwest.
6.5	Fourmile Lake and dam. The Rye Spur-Badger Lake summer hiking trail crosses to the east of the dam. Proceed west through the campground along the lake shore.

6.7   Intersection with the Fourmile Lake Road (No. 3661), and the road to the Squaw Lakes Trail. Proceed south, up the hill, if you wish to complete the loop to your starting point. This portion of the Fourmile Lake Trail is described in another section.

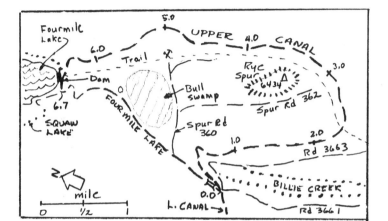

H6. FOURMILE LAKE

Trail Difficulty: Intermediate
                       on Forest Service road

Starting Point: Intersection of FS roads 3650, 3661
                       and 3633. MP 2.4 on Lower Canal Trail
                       elevation 5660'

Trail Length: 2.6 miles to Fourmile Lake, one way

Elevation Change: Gain of 260 feet to mile 2.0, then
                       loss of 176 feet to Fourmile Lake

Maps: USGS: Lake of the Woods (15 min.)
                       USFS: Winema NF; The Sky Lakes Area;
                              Jackson Klamath Winter Trails

   The better access to this trail is from State Highway 140 to
the south by either the Lower Canal Trail (2.4 miles) or by the
Billie Creek Trail (3.0 miles), the former providing the easiest
access. This trail can be skied as a loop using the Upper Canal
Trail; however, the most popular route is to continue from the
Lower Canal Trail and then return over the same route. On a good
day with a broken trail, I have skied in on this latter route
from Highway 140 in 90 minutes and back in 60 minutes.

   The Fourmile Lake Trail follows FS Road 3661, which is also
used by snowmobiles coming from the lower portion of Rd 3661 or
Rd 3633. I try to ski this trail during the morning hours as
snowmobile traffic usually does not start until the afternoon.
The trail has several hills and valleys, and passes numerous
small lakes, making it a challenging and an interesting route.
Since the trail is fairly open and exposed to the south, on a
warm sunny day snow conditions can change drastically from
morning to afternoon.

Mile   Description

0.0   Start by taking the road marked with the yellow
           snowmobile signs on the north side of the inter-
           section, and cross the Cascade Canal.   The trail
           climbs for a short distance, descends into a
           small valley, climbs another hill, and descends
           into a second valley.

0.7   Near the bottom of the second valley, FS spur

road No. 360 begins to the north east, leading along
the southern edge of Bull Swamp. You can proceed
along this spur road for about 1.1 mile to a rock
quarry, or 2.5 miles along roads No. 360 and 362
to the southwest side of Rye Spur.

The trail then passes on the west side of Bull
Swamp with many small ponds, and on the east
side of Lake Janice. Bull Swamp is a favorate
place for snowmobilers to play.

1.5   Pass between Lake Bernice (on the left) and
       Lake Clovis (on the right) after the trail
       bears around a curve to the right and up a slight
       hill.

2.0   High point at elevation 5920 feet. The trail
       descends to Fourmile Lake, passing Lake Aphis
       (on the left), and then steepens through several
       switchbacks.

2.6   Fourmile Lake. Intersection with the Squaw Lakes
       Road and Trail. If you turn right (to the east),
       and ski through the campground, you will reach
       the Fourmile Lake dam. This is also the start
       of the 6.5-mile loop trip along the Upper Canal
       Trail back to the intersection where you started.

       This is a good spot to have lunch, as several picnic
       tables are available in the campground. All you
       have to do is clean off the snow to find a place to
       sit.

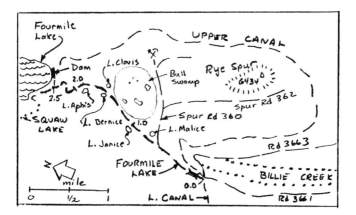

H7. POWERLINE

Trail Difficulty:	Beginning to intermediate on logging and powerline roads
Starting Point:	Intersection of Lower Canal Trail at mile 0.3 from Highway 140; elevation 5150'
Trail Length:	2.9 miles (4.7 km) to Jct with Highway 140 and Road No. 3661
Elevation Change:	Gain of 70 feet to mile 0.5, then loss of 220 feet to Jct with Highway 140
Maps:	USGS: Lake of the Woods (15 min.) USFS: Winema NF; The Sky Lakes Area; Jackson Klamath Winter Trails

This trail, which parallels State Highway 140, is accessed from either end at Sno-Park areas. For most of the distance it is fairly sheltered by dense timber. The trail can be used as part of a loop trip with the Lower Canal and Billie Creek Trails, a total distance of 8.3 miles (13.4 km). It is also the extension of the Lake of the Woods Trail connecting to the resort at the east end. Half of the trail follows a logging spur road and the other half follows a powerline road, the latter made more difficult by a rocky and irregular surface. There is an extremely steep section, several hundred feet long, at the end of the spur road where it connects to the powerline road. An alternate route is being planned along the powerline to avoid this steep section.

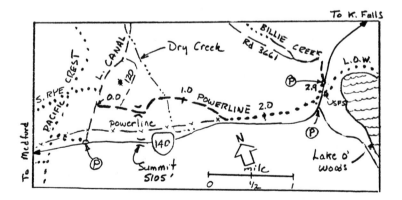

Mile	Description
0.0	Start at the junction with the Lower Canal Trail, 0.3 miles northeast of the Sno-Park area. The first portion follows spur Road No. 050, climbing slightly.
0.2	A skid road comes in from the north. This is part of the loop from the Lower Canal Trail starting with spur Road No. 120.
0.5	The highest point on the trail at a small saddle: elevation 5220'. From this point the trail curves to the left, losing elevation and crossing Dry Creek. Proceed through a large clear-cut area with a spectacular view of Mt. McLoughlin.

The trail climbs to a second high point and then deteriorates into a skid road. At the end, the trail drops sharply to the powerline through a series of turns. Fallen timber and the steepness will require you to sidestep or traverse the slope. There are plans to make this drop less severe. |
| 1.5 | End spur road and start along the powerline road. The powerline can be skied back to the Lower Canal Trail, intersecting it 0.1 mile northeast of the Sno-Park area. State Highway 140 can be seen below the trail.

Proceed ahead along the powerline on a south-facing slope. The trail has an irregular profile with many interesting ups and downs. |
2.7	Intersection with snowmobile route from the east Sno-Park which connects across Highway 140 to the west-side road along Lake of the Woods. From this point skiers and snowmobilers share the route, so be careful. A parking area is available for about 10 cars on the south side of the highway.
2.8	You can cross the highway at this point and travel east along the Lake of the Woods Trail to the lodge 1.5 miles (2.4 km) away. The trail goes between the buildings of the Forest Service ranger station.
2.9	Intersection with State Highway 140, Road No. 3661, and the start of the Billie Creek Trail. Parking is available for about 10 cars. Sno-Park permits are required.

Trail Difficulty:	Intermediate on trail
Starting Point:	1) Spur Road 900, 0.7 mile east of Fish Lake Resort; elevation 4680'; or 2) Pacific Crest Trail, 0.2 mile south of Highway 140; elevation 5000'
Trail Length:	1.5 mile (2.4 km)
Elevation Change:	Gain of 320' to Pacific Crest Trail
Maps:	USGS: Mt. McLoughlin (15 min.) USFS: Rogue River NF; Jackson Klamath Winter Trails

This trail, little used, links Fish Lake Resort and the Pacific Crest Trail. Fortunately it is well marked with the standard blue diamonds, as it would be difficult to follow otherwise. A double braze on trees is also used to mark the trail. It parallels State Highway 140 along the north flank of Mt. McLoughlin, through dense woods and adjacent to open areas of recent lava flows. Skiing west and downhill from the Pacific Crest Trail, several steep and narrow sections are encountered; however the trail is primarily in the intermediate range requiring step turns and snow plowing.

The trail description is from east to west, but easy access can be gained from either end. It is also part of a 6.4-mile (10.3-km) loop trip using Lollipop, Lund's Link, South Rye and the Pacific Crest trails. You can also reach this trail from the Lower Canal Trail Sno-Park by skiing west to the Pacific Crest Trail parallel to Highway 140 and then skiing south across the highway.

Mile   Description

                  Access is gained from State Highway 140 just west of the Jackson-Klamath Co. line. A Pacific Crest Trail sign is visible just off the highway at the end of a large through cut. Proceed along the Pacific Crest Trail to the south for about 0.2 mile, crossing a small skid road.

0.0	The intersection with the Pacific Crest Trail is marked with engraved wooden signs for hikers. The ski trail is marked with blue diamonds. Proceed west at this point.
0.3	State Highway 140 is visible and vehicle traffic heard across a large open lava flow.
1.2	A steep section descends along the south side of a hill.
1.5	Exit through dense timber onto spur Road No.900. This is also mile 1.0 on the Lollipop Trail. Cross this road and follow the trail through the woods, 0.7 mile to Fish Lake Resort and 1.0 mile to the Fish Lake Sno-Park.

If you are skiing this trail uphill from Fish Lake, the beginning is a little hard to find. It is marked with a small engraved sign on a short post: "TRAIL". The trail starts in dense timber across spur Road No. 900, just opposite the trail from Fish Lake Lodge at the northeast end of Fish Lake.

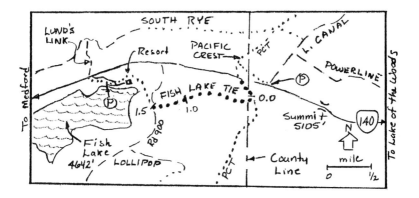

H9. SOUTH RYE

Trail Difficulty:	Beginning to intermediate on road Intermediate to advanced on trail
Starting Point:	Sno-Park on Highway 140, 1.2 miles west of Fish Lake junction; elevation 4660'
Trail Length:	4.0 miles (6.4 km) to Jct with Lower Canal Trail
Elevation Change:	Gain of 420 feet to Jct with the Pacific Crest Trail
Maps:	USGS: Mt. McLoughlin (15 min.) USFS: Rogue River NF; Jackson Klamath Winter Trails

This trail parallels the north side of State Highway 140. It can be accessed from either end, the east-west direction providing a good downhill run. The west half of the trail is on a Forest Service road and the east half is an improved trail. Only the east half is marked with the standard blue diamonds, and is the most difficult with several short steep and narrow sections. Skiing the trail only one way requires leaving a car at the west end and at the Sno-Park for the Lower Canal Trailhead. A somewhat strenuous loop trip follows the Pacific Crest Trail, the Fish Lake Tie Trail, and then through the Fish Lake Campground and access road system. An alternative is to return along the powerline between the South Rye Trail and Highway 140. A new trail, Lund's Link, connects the Fish Lake Sno-Park and Resort with mile 1.4 on the trail - allowing a shorter 6.4-mile (10.3-km) loop trip.

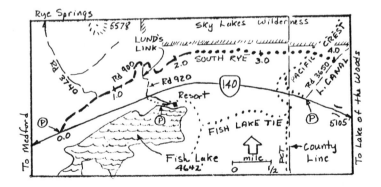

| Mile | Description |

0.0   Start at the west end at the Rye Springs Sno-Park (Road No. 3740) on the north side of Highway 140. There is room for approximately 6 cars. A sign post clearly marks the start of the trail and a single page, large scale map is usually available in aplastic bag attached to the sign.

Proceed up the road, crossing the power line, a cattle guard and a guard-rail barrier. This portion of the trail is not marked with the blue diamonds. The road climbs steeply.

0.7   Intersection with spur Road No. 900. Road No. 3740 continues uphill to the left to Rye Springs. It is 1.6 miles to Rye Springs along this road, mostly on the level. A spectacular view is provided of Mt. McLoughlin at 1.4 miles. Snowmobiles may use the road to this point when travelling to Rye Springs.

Take the road to the right. At this point the road is fairly level and tree lined. Occasional openings over lava flows provide a view of Brown Mountain to the southeast.

1.4   Proceed around a small stream valley and pass by the intersection with spur road 920 (Lund's Link Trail) on an outside curve. This trail connects to Highway 140, approximately 0.6 mile (1.0 km) downhill and to the Fish Lake Sno-Park 0.9 mile (1.5 km). The trail then continues through another inside curve and climbs slightly.

2.1   The road ends and the improved trail starts. Proceed sharp left and then immediately right at the end of the road. From this point on, the trail is marked with blue diamonds and the cross-country skier sign.

The trail proceeds through the woods with many ups and downs and lots of opportunity to practice step turns. The net effect is to climb. Tree-less lava flows provide occasional open areas. If you are skiing east to west, there are several difficult downhill section along this part. Generally these can be avoided by traversing; how-ever I did notice where one skier had walked down every one of these.

3.4   A three-foot diameter Pine tree marked as a bearing

tree looms almost in the middle of the trail. This
tree references the common corner to Sections 25, 30
and 36. This is also the north-south boundary
between the Rogue River and Winema National Forests,
and Jackson and Klamath Counties. The trail climbs
to a flat ridgeline.

3.6   Intersection with the Pacific Crest Trail which is
        identified by several blue arrows and diamonds
        nailed to a tree. It is approximately one mile
        south to Highway 140 along the unmarked trail.

        The South Rye Trail continues east guided by blue
        diamonds attached to burned snags. It opens out
        onto a hill where Brown Mountain dominates with
        Mt. Ashland ski area seen in the distance.
        Proceed down this hill and into the trees.

4.0   Cross the Cascade Canal ditch and intersect the
        Lower Canal Trail. The Sno-Park area on Highway
        140 is 0.5 mile south along this trail (Rd. 3650).

Trail Difficulty:	Intermediate on trail and spur road
Starting Point:	Fish Lake Sno-Park adjacent to the Fish Lake Resort; elevation 4650'
Trail Length:	0.9 mile (1.5 km), one way
Elevation Change:	Gain of 390'
Maps:	USGS: Mt. McLoughlin (15 min.)
	USFS: Rogue River National Forest; Jackson Klamath Winter Trails

This short connecting link crosses a wooded area, hence the name Lund, meaning a grove of trees in the Scandinavian languages. The link allows a loop trip from Fish Lake Resort using South Rye, Pacific Crest, Fish Lake Tie and Lollipop trails. The 6.5 mile (10.5 km) loop can be skied in either direction, providing a variety of terrain.

Start from the Fish Lake Sno-Park on the north shore of Fish Lake, also the trailhead for the Lollipop Trail which is 0.3 mile west of Fish Lake Resort. The trail climbs to Highway 140 and crosses just west of the entrance to the resort. It then connects to spur Road No. 900, the South Rye Trail. This portion of the trail is steep, requiring control coming downhill. The trail is marked with the standard blue diamonds.

Mile	Description
0.0	Start from the trailhead at the west end of the Fish Lake Sno-Park. Ski north through the campground and cross the snowmobile trail. Climb towards Highway 140 on an old road.
0.1	Ski below and parallel to the access road on a trail. It goes slightly downhill and then uphill and crosses the unplowed Doe Point Road.
0.3	Cross Highway 140 about 100' west of the entrance to the resort.
	Ski north and uphill on USFS spur Road No. 920
0.4	The trail splits. The one to the right eventually follows the powerline east. Take the left branch and go through a stock gate. Continue uphill.

There is one short level portion and a sharp switchback at the halfway point. There are several steep sections.

0.9   Junction with South Rye Trail, spur Road No. 900 at mile 1.4. Coming down the South Rye Trail, you may have trouble identifying this intersection. It is on an outside curve between two inside curves, and partially hidden behind a five-foot high mound of rock and soil. If it is not buried by snow, a No. 920 sign may be visible. A trailhead sign should be visible.

It is 0.5 mile downhill left to the Rye Springs Road and 1.4 miles to Highway 140. It is 0.7 mile to the right to the end of spur road No. 900, and 2.2 miles to the Pacific Crest Trail.

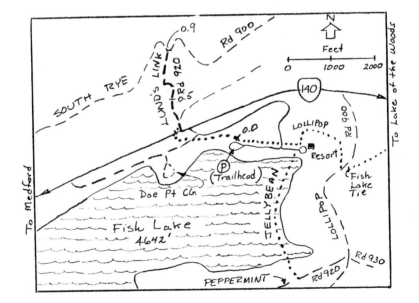

H11. LOLLIPOP

Trail Difficulty:	Beginnin to intermediate: on road and trail
Starting Point:	Fish Lake Sno-Park, 0.3 miles west of the resort; elevation 4660'
Trail Length:	6.8 miles (10.9 km) round trip
Elevation Change:	Gain of 340 feet to approximate half-way point
Maps:	USGS: Mt. McLoughlin (15 min.) USFS: Rogue River NF; Jackson Klamath Winter Trails

Lollipop is part of a system consisting of interconnected trails with equally unusual names: Jellybean, Peppermint, and Candy "Cain". These trails, except for a short section of Peppermint are easy and enjoyable to ski, with spectacular views of Mt. McLoughlin and Brown Mountain along the way. A nice feature is that the routes start and end near Fish Lake Lodge, a great place for eating, drinking and relaxing. A restroom is open in the campground near the trailhead.

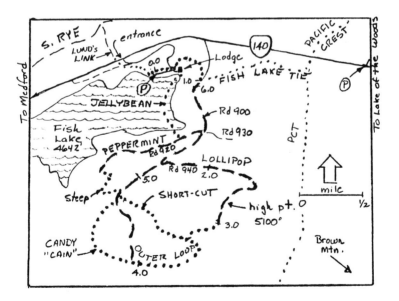

Lollipop can be skied clockwise or counterclockwise, and interwoven with side trips on the other trails. The clockwise route will be described below. All trails are marked with blue diamonds and large descriptive trail signs at key junctions. A detailed Forest Service trail map is available at the trailhead, and Sno-Park permits are available at the Lodge.

Mile	Description
0.0	Parking for 20 cars is available at the Sno-Park on the edge of Fish Lake to the west of the Lodge. Parking at the Lodge is reserved for customers. Start at the large bulletin board and follow the marked trail through the campground, behind the restrooms, and cross the entrance road.
0.3	Lodge area - turn north and ski between the restrooms and the residence.
	The trail turns east and goes through a campground, then up a small hill, turning south through the woods. Watch for snowmachines, as this is a shared trail to mile 1.2.
1.0	Exit from the trees onto spur Road No. 900, approximately 0.4 miles south of State Highway 140. The start of the Fish Lake Tie Trail is across the road.
	Proceed south around the east end of Fish Lake along spur Road No. 900. The new Inter-resort Snowmachine Route from Lake of the Woods will enter somewhere along this road.
1.2	Intersection with Peppermint Trail (spur Road No. 920) to the right. Road No. 930, to the left, leads to the lower slopes of Brown Mountain, ending in a lava field a short distance east. Snowmobiles are allowed to drive to this point.
	Take the center road, go through an open gate and start climbing up a gradual hill (just think of the nice run back).
1.6	The end of the stem and the start of the Lollipop loop. If you wish to ski clockwise (the recommended direction), turn left and proceed up the hill (spur Road No. 940). This is the steepest part of the trail. Even though the trail climbs steadily, you are rewarded with a spectacular

view of Mt. McLoughlin to the north.

2.5   The road makes a sharp U-turn to the west and
levels off. From here it proceeds west and then
south climbing to the high point. Another good
view of McLoughlin.

2.8   High point at elevation 5100 feet.

3.0   After a short run downhill, the trail makes an
abrupt right turn to the west. This junction is
not well marked, since the area has recently been
clear cut. Do not continue straight ahead. The
trail now follows a trail through the woods.

3.3   Split in the Lollipop Trail. A short-cut back
to the Lodge turns off to the right. It proceeds
0.7 mile west where it ties back into the outer
loop of the Lollipop Trail (saving almost one mile).

Turn left for the longer outer loop and ski down
hill. The trail follows around the outer edge
of the clearcut. Brown Mountain is to the east.
One last downhill section brings the trail to
the upper end of spur Road No. 900.

The snow covered hills, brushpiles, and tree
stumps in this open area provide some interesting
mogels and slopes to practice turns and straight
downhill running.

4.1   Intersection with spur Road No. 900 and Candy
"Cain" Trail. The return to the Lodge goes
right (north) and Candy "Cain" goes straight
ahead (west).

The return along Road No. 900 is a gradual uphill
climb.

4.6   The other end of Candy "Cain" Trail intersects
from the left.

4.7   High point on the return road (elev. 4930').

4.8   Intersection with the Lollipop short-cut on the
right. The Peppermint Trail is about 100 feet
ahead on the left. It follows along the edge
of the clearning on the left and then goes into
the woods about 500 feet below the road.

Start downhill on a nice gradual run.

5.2	Intersection with the loop and stem of the Lollipop. You are now back at the beginning of the loop (mile 1.6). Return to the Lodge and Sno-Park over the same trail.
6.5	Fish Lake Lodge.
6.8	Fish Lake Sno-Park.

H12. JELLYBEAN

This 0.6-mile (1.0-km) long beginning trail crosses the east end of Fish Lake. It starts at the Fish Lake trailer park to the east of the Lodge and ends on the Peppermint Trail, 0.2 mile west of the intersection with Lollipop Trail. If the ice on the lake is unsafe, follow a route along the shore. The south 0.1 mile portion of the trail is in the woods and is clearly marked with blue diamonds, otherwise there are no trail markings along the lake. The trail is at lake elevation and can provide an easy loop trip with the east 0.2 mile of the Peppermint Trail, returning by way of the Lollipop Trail, a two-mile round trip.

H13. PEPPERMINT

This 1.4-mile (2.2-km) long advanced trail connects with the west loop of the Lollipop Trail. It starts at mile 1.2 on the Lollipop Trail and proceeds west along spur Road No. 920. The Jellybean Trail intersects after 0.2 mile on the right. The trail climbs slightly along this spur road. At 0.9 mile from the start, just before encountering a metal gate, the trail turns sharply left and climbs through the woods. This is the most difficult portion of the trail, requiring side-stepping or herring-bone technique to climb or snow plow to descend. After climbing through the woods for 0.5 mile with a 200-foot elevation gain, the trail exits on a clear-cut just below the Lollipop Trail. A trail sign is posted here. Proceed along the edge of the clearing to the road just below the short-cut for the Lollipop Trail (mile 4.8).

The Peppermint Trail can be skied as a loop with various portions of the Lollipop Trail, either clockwise or counterclockwise.

H14. CANDY "CAIN"

This trail forms a short 0.7-mile (1.1-km) loop with the west
leg of the Lollipop Trail. One end is at mile 4.1 and the other
at mile 4.6. From either end, the trail drops slightly over 100
feet to the midpoint and follows along the edge of a recent
clear-cut. The trail provides an easy downhill run and climb.
It is named after an extremely active and former president of the
Grants Pass Nordic Club.

H15. BROWN MOUNTAIN

Trail Difficulty:	Intermediate to advanced
Starting Point:	Sno-Park on Highway 140 at the junction of USFS Road No. 3650 (Lower Canal Trail), 0.6 miles west of the summit; elevation 5050'
Trail Length:	2.5 miles (4.0 km), one way
Elevation Change:	Gain of 2260' to the summit
Maps:	USGS: Mt. McLoughlin (15 min.) USFS: Winema National Forest; Rogue River National Forest; Jackson Klamath Winter Trails

There are no established trails on Brown Mountain, so you are free to make your own. The slopes of this mountain attract the mountaineering and telemark skiers who like a good downhill run. The preferred location and the easiest access is the north face with a 25% slope. Skiing on this shield volcano is similar to skiing on Pelican Butte, and also has many open areas. The summit has a small classic volcanic crater, and fumarolic hot spots have been identified on the north side. Many skiers use climbing skins to attack the mountain, and a downhill, mountain, or telemark binding to enjoy the run back.

The best parking area is at the Lower Canal Trailhead Sno-Park on the north side of Highway 140. Cross the highway and ski east about one-half mile before starting uphill. From here it is about 2.0 miles to the top; however you can enjoy any portion of the slope, depending upon you ability. There is a beautiful view of Mt. McLoughlin to the northwest, Fish Lake to the west and Lake of the Woods to the east.

The Inter-resort Snowmachine Trail between Lake of the Woods and Fish Lake will open the winter of 1987-88. This 14-foot wide trail will cross the lower north flank of the mountain.

I. KLAMATH WEST

West of Klamath Falls are two interesting and challenging ski areas: Hamaker and Chase Mountains - Bear Valley, and Mountain Lakes Wilderness. Both of these are approximately 30 minutes from Klamath Falls, and a little over one hour from the Rogue Valley cities.

The Hamaker and Chase Mountains - Bear Valley can be a short half-day trip with both challenging downhill and easy cross country available. Bear Valley, in the middle of the winter, has the added attraction of being a Bald Eagle nesting area. Mountain Lakes Wilderness requires more planning as it involves longer trips, with skiers often spending the night in this wilderness area. Three different trailheads allow access from State Highways 66 and 140.

If you enjoy urban skiing, Moore Park on the south shore of Upper Klamath Lake offers a variety of trails. For the beginner, there are many gentle slopes on the open area behind the tennis courts. There are also several loop trail in the main park area that follow a road system. One of these loops climbs to an overlook of the lake. A third trail goes south along a ridge above Link River. You can follow jeep roads to Riverside School or climb KAGO Hill. From KAGO Hill, there are a number of jeep roads that go up the numerous canyons to the west - one loops around and reaches a summit above Moore Park. From Riverside School, you can ski down to the Link River and follow the nature trail along the west bank of the canyon.

I1. HAMAKER AND CHASE MOUNTAIN - BEAR VALLEY

Trail Difficulty: Beginning to advanced

Starting Point: On access road to Chase Mountain Lookout,
                         1.2 miles west of Keno on Highway 66;
                         elevation 4335' at Highway 66

Trail Length: 1.0 to 8.0 miles (1.9 - 12.9 km)
                         one way

Elevation Change: Gain of 2230' to top of Hamaker Mtn.

Maps: USGS: Klamath Falls (15 min.)

A skier has two choices; (1) driving to the saddle between
Chase and Hamaker Mountains or to the top of Hamaker Mountain and
doing some fast downhill running, or (2) driving part way up and
skiing down Bear Valley towards Worden on US Highway 97. The
latter can be especially enjoyable in February and March when
Bald Eagles are nesting and feeding.

The road to the top of Hamaker Mountain is open in the winter
since it provides access to an aircraft control station. There
is a fire lookout on the top of Chase Mountain. The trip can be
as difficult as you want to make it. The Bear Valley route is
the easiest with a fairly flat grade.

The trail description refers to the distance up the Chase
Mountain Road from State Highway 66. Note that it is unlawful to
ski, snowmobile or park on the roadway.

Mile   Description

0.0   Junction with Highway 66, 1.2 mile west of Keno.
           Drive up a road with many switchbacks.

1.6   Metal building on left with a parking area just
           beyond. You can ski on an unimproved road southeast
           about 0.6 mile to a small lake - elevation 4800'.

2.4   Top of an intermediate hill. A road off to the left
           drops down into Bear Valley. No parking available.

2.8   Bottom of hill. The Bear Valley Trail starts to the
           left through the trees. There is an open meadow to
           the southeast with an unimproved road running along
           the southwest. Ski on the road for about 8.0 miles
           down Bear Valley to Worden on US Highway 97. This

174

trail starts at 4800' and drops to 4100'. There is a narrow canyon with many Aspen trees along the mid-point of the trail.

Continue driving uphill.

3.5 Deadend road to the left down to a small government building.

5.7 Saddle between Chase and Hamaker mountains. You can park here and ski northwest up Chase Mountain to the fire lookout - a 500-foot climb; or ski downhill northeast to Bear Valley; or continue driving up Hamaker Mountain.

Parking is available on the right. Two roads lead off to the north (right). The one to the left leads around the back side of Chase Mountain; the one on the right climbs to the lookout. Continue driving uphill.

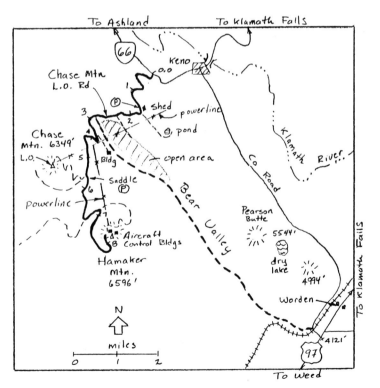

6.8   Road leads off to the left. This is an intermediate
point to access the slopes of Hamaker Mountain and
a powerline opening. No parking is available.

8.2   Top of Hamaker Mountain with the aircraft control
station. A fence surrounds the site and entrance
is restricted. There is a turn-around available for
parking. You can ski around the fence to the left
and intersect a powerline opening. It is a steep
run from here down to the saddle or Bear Valley - the
latter about 1.5 to 2.0 miles away, depending on how
steep you want to ski. You can be picked up at the
saddle or lower on the access road and make another
trip. The powerline opening is the most popular run;
however it is narrow and steep.

I2-I5. MOUNTAIN LAKES WILDERNESS

The Mountain Lakes Wilderness consists of a full township of land (36 square miles) between Upper Klamath Lake and Lake of the Woods. It is the remains of a massive composite volcano which towered over 12,000 feet and covered approximately 85 square miles, one of the largest in the southern Cascades. Collapse of the summit forming a caldera, similar to the formation of Crater Lake, and subsequent glaciation left only portions of the former mountain. A series of eruptions along the flanks of the caldera formed promient peaks such as as Aspen Butte, Mt. Carmine and Mt. Harriman. The glaciation and other erosive forces prevented formation of a large lake within the rim, thus many small glacial lakes or tarns were formed. The largest and most popular lake is Lake Harriette, located in the center of the wilderness.

At one time there were five trails into the wilderness, but this has been reduced to three maintained trails: Varney Creek (from the north), Mt. Lakes (from the west) and Clover Creek (from the south). These all connect to the Mountain Lakes Loop Trail, No. 3727, which traces a 8.6-mile (13.8-km) loop around the remains of the caldera rim.

Most of the wilderness is above 6,000 feet, with Lake Harriette at 6760 feet, and the highest point, Aspen Butte, at 8208 feet.

Skiing into the area requires a longer trip than hiking in the summer, as the Forest Service access roads are usually snow covered. Fortunately most of the trails have fairly gentle grades, with only three significant climbs on the Loop Trail. The area is not signed for winter trips, thus you must depend upon your navigational skills, tree blazes and an occassional sign.

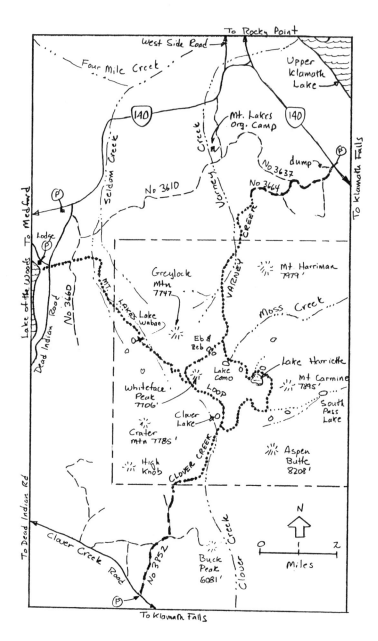

Trail Difficulty:	Advanced on road and trail
Starting Point:	On Highway 140 at USFS Road No. 3637, 3.3 miles southeast of the junction with the Westside Road to Rocky Point; elevation 4170'
Trail Length:	7.3 miles (11.7 km) to junction with Loop Trail, one way [3.8 miles (6.1 km) on trail only]
Elevation Change:	Gain of 2600' (1220' on trail only)
Maps:	USGS: Lake of the Woods (15 min.) USFS: Winema National Forest; Mountain Lakes Wilderness

The is the shortest and most popular trail into the wilderness area. Your starting point in the winter will vary, depending upon snow conditions. Usually you can drive part way on USFS Road No. 3637, thus eliminating some of the distance and climb (the portion of the trail on the road is the steepest of the entire trip). An alternate starting point is to drive in on USFS Road No. 3610 towards the Mountain Lakes Organizational Camp. The road junction is on Highway 140 approximately one mile west of the junction with the Westside Road. Varney Creek crosses Road No. 3610 just beyond the camp, about 1.7 miles from the junction with Highway 140. Following it up the creek for approximately 2.5 miles will then intersect the new trail. This older trail followed the east bank of Varney Creek.

Mile	Description
0.0	Road junction with Highway 140 and USFS Road No. 3637. There is limited parking here, so do not block the road as this is also the access to a county dump. Ski southwest on level terrain.
0.1	Road to the county dump goes off to the right.
0.4	Spur road goes off to the left - keep right and start climbing.
1.5	Junction with USFS Road No. 3664. Takes this road to the left and climb steeply. A sign

for the trailhead should be visible.

1.9   Spur road takes off to the left - keep right and
        head west around a ridge.

3.5   End of road at a large turn around. A view is
        provided to the southeast from this saddle area.
        The summer trail starts on the right and heads
        southwest.

        The trails goes through dense woods following
        the contour around the hill. Look for tree blazes.

4.7   Wilderness boundary - sign on left.

4.9   Cross Varney Creek on a wooden bridge. There is a
        small camp site here. The older trail from the
        organizational camp comes in at this point along
        the east bank (it may be difficult to locate).

        Continue along the west bank of the stream, climbing
        at a 5% grade. You will traverse several open area,
        usually on the upper edge.

6.1   Cross Varney Creek.

6.9   Reach a high point, elevation 6780', on a small
        saddle. Start downhill.

7.3   Intersection with the Mountain Lakes Loop Trail.
        To the right and uphill 0.3 mile are Eb and Zeb
        Lakes, and to left 0.4 mile is Lake Como, and 1.5
        miles is Lake Harriette.

        See the description on the Mountain Lakes Loop
        Trail for more details.

I3. CLOVER CREEK

Trail Difficulty: Advanced on road and trail

Starting Point: Clover Creek Road at junction of
                          USFS Road No. 3852, 6.0 miles east
                          of Dean Indian Road and 0.5 mile
                          west of Winema National Forest
                          boundary; elevation 4840'

Trail Length: 5.2 miles (8.4 km) to Loop Trail
                          [2.1 miles (3.4 km) on trail only]

Maps: USGS: Lake of the Woods (15 min.)
                          USFS: Winema National Forest;
                                 Mountain Lakes Wilderness

   This trail approaches the wilderness area from the south. The
Clover Creek Road connecting Keno and Dead Indian Road, is
usually kept open in the winter. Access Road No. 3852 is the
Buck Peak Road and is also used by snowmobilers. The climb to
this 6081-foot summit is also a good side trip, providing a view
of the surrounding area. Depending upon snow conditions, the
trips can be started at any point on Road No. 3852, thus
shortening the trip. The summer trailhead is at the wilderness
boundary. The first 0.7 mile of the trail inside the wilderness
boundary is new and thus is not marked with tree blazes. This
makes following the trail more difficult.

Mile   Description

0.0   Start from the Clover Creek Road and head due north.
             Parking is limited along the shoulder of the road.
             The trail climbs gradually.

1.2   The trail turns to the east, climbing at a steeper
             rate.

1.6   The Buck Peak Road, spur No. 190 goes east - turn
             north and continue on Road No. 3852.

2.4   Split in the road - take the right branch and ski
             to the right of a small hill, still heading north.

3.1   The summer trail head and the wilderness boundary.
             The trail turns to the east.

3.8   Intersect Clover Creek - stay on the west bank.
             Ski north up a 15% grade - tree blazes start.

5.0	Ski by a series of small ponds and cross Clover Creek.
5.2	Intersection with the Mountain Lakes Loop Trail.

Clover Lake is 0.1 mile straight ahead. Lake Harriette is 3.4 miles to the right.

I4. MOUNTAIN LAKES

Trail Difficulty:	Advanced on trail
Starting Point:	Lake of the Wood Resort parking area; elevation 5000'
Trail Length:	5.8 miles (9.3 km) to Loop Trail, one way
Elevation Change:	2360' gain
Maps:	USGS: Lake of the Woods (15 min.) USFS: Winema National Forest; Mountain Lakes Wilderness

This trail has also been called the Seldom Creek Trail, as it follows this drainage for about half of the trip. The trail is the longest into the Mountain Lakes Wilderness, if the road access is not considered on the other two. It has the advantage of starting from a resort area where ample parking is available.

Mile	Description
0.0	The trail start approximately 500 feet southeast of the Lake of the Woods Lodge area, opposite the rest rooms near the Sunset Trail. A sign marks the beginning of the trail: "Mt. Lakes Spur Trail 3721". Ski east through the woods - the trail is marked with tree blazes.
	An alternate starting point is to park in the Sno-Park near the junction of Highway 140 and Dead Indian Road, ski east to USFS Road No. 3660, and then ski up it 1.2 miles to where the trail crosses.
0.1	Cross Lake of the Woods access road.
0.4	Cross Dead Indian Road - begin climbing.
1.2	Cross USFS Road No. 3660 - marked with a sign: "7 miles to Lakes Eb and Zeb" and "8 miles to Clover Lake."
1.8	Intersect Seldom Creek. Ski south parallel to the creek, crossing it several times. The trail approaches 10% for the next mile.

3.0	Wilderness boundary.
4.0	Lake Wahan is about 500' south of the trail. Greylock Mountain looms to the east.
4.5	The trail leaves Seldom Creek and climbs through a series of switchbacks, continuing at 15% grade.
5.8	Saddle between Crater Mountain ridge and Whiteface Peak. Intersection with the Mountain Lakes Loop Trail.

Lakes Eb and Zeb are 1.3 miles to the left through a second saddle and then downhill. Clover Lake is 1.5 miles to the right and also downhill.

I5. MOUNTAIN LAKES LOOP

Trail Difficulty:	Advanced (very difficult)
Starting Point:	At end of any of the three trails leading into Mountain Lakes Wilderness: Varney Creek, Clover Creek or Mountain Lakes; elevation varies
Trail Length:	8.6 miles (13.8 km)
Elevation Change:	Low point: 6640', high point 7520'
Maps:	USGS: Lake of the Woods (15 min.) USFS: Winema National Forest; Mountain Lakes Wilderness

The Loop Trail is the most difficult of any trail in the Mountain Lakes Wilderness, as it does not follow any drainage valley. Instead it follows the rim of the caldera, with many ups and downs. It also is a problem with exposure to wind and snow drifts. It is very difficult to follow in the winter, even with the tree blazes. The description will run clockwise starting from the end of the Varney Creek Trail.

Mile   Description

0.0   End of the Varney Creek Trail at elevation 6140', low point on the loop. Turn left to the south on a level grade.

0.8   Lake Como to the south. Ski west and start to climb.

1.3   Lake Zepplin can been seen through the trees. It is contained by a rocky dam, called "pro-rampart talus" - material slid over a snow pack. The trail climbs steeply up the west slope of a hill.

1.7   A saddle, elevation 6920' - a beautiful view is provided of Lake Harriette.

1.9   Lake Harriette and the intersection of the old Moss Creek Trail. Echo Lake is just below on this trail. Elevation 6760'.

           Circle around the north and east side of the lake and then begin a steep climb up to another saddle.

Mount Carmine looms to the southeast.

3.2   Saddle, elevation 7320'. The South Pass Trail turns off to the left and east. It is 1.5 miles downhill to this lake. Turn right and continue climbing.

3.5   Intersection with the Aspen Butte Trail (seen to the south), and high point on the trail at 7520'. Swing northwest and start down hill.

4.2   The trail turns southwest, still heading down hill.

5.3   Intersection with the Clover Creek Trail; elevation 6640'. Turn north and start uphill.

5.4   Clover Lake on the left.

5.8   Turn northwest and follow the contour of the hill. The trail then begins to climb at 15%.

6.9   Intersection with the Mountain Lakes Trail, just below Whiteface Peak; elevation 7360.

            Turn north around the west edge of Whiteface Peak.

7.3   A saddle at elevation 7420'. Turn east and start downhill at 25%.

8.2   Pass between Lakes Eb and Zeb.

8.6   Intersection with the Varney Creek Trail; elevation 6140'

J. BUCK PRAIRIE

The only cross-country ski area in southern Oregon managed by the Bureau of Land Management, this system consists of almost 20 miles of interconnected trails on public and private land between Dead Indian Road and Hyatt Prairie Road. The two trailheads, Dead Indian Road Summit and Campers Cove, are 15 and 25 miles respectively east of Ashland in the southern Cascades.

The Dead Indian Road Summit, elevation 5180', is the most popular access. Ample parking is available and the trailhead is clearly marked. The Campers Cove access (elevation 5020') on the southwest shore of Hyatt Reservoir is seldom used and poorly marked; however, a store and restaurant do provide a welcome service.

The trails generally run north-south, climbing to 6000' along a ridge and with views of Ashland and the Siskiyou Mountains to the west, and Buck Prairie, Mt. McLoughlin, Brown Mountain, and Mountain Lakes Wilderness to the east. The trails are marked with the standard blue diamonds as well as orange diamonds with black arrows. The orange diamonds, the same used for snowmobile trails, indicate major turns on the ski trails. Unfortunately, several of the trails are marked only for one direction of travel, making them difficult to follow in the opposite direction. The non-uniformity in signing and the many interconnected trails, are confusing, even with a map. Two major trail junctions have a special sign to assist skiers, and there is an outhouse one mile in from Dead Indian Road. The BLM district office in Medford plans to improve the trail signing, thus there may be changes from my detailed descriptions. A trail map is available at the Dead Indian Road Summit.

The ski trails follow both BLM roads and trails, with some overlap with snowmobile trails from the south. The highest point in the vicinity is Table Mountain, elevation 6113', with a fire lookout. It is fairly easy climb to this viewpoint. In addition, there are numerous open meadows to practice downhill skiing and telemark turns.

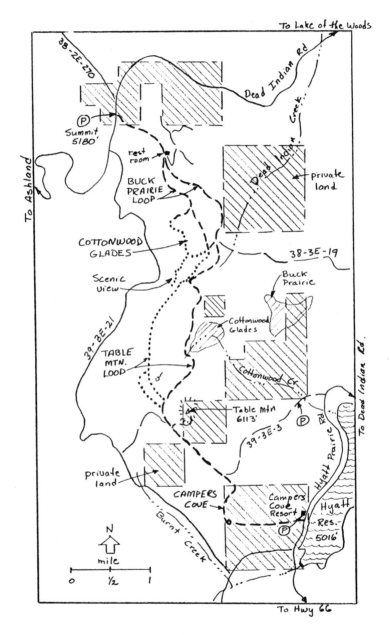

J1. BUCK PRAIRIE LOOP

Trail Difficulty:	Beginning on road and trail
Starting Point:	Dead Indian Road Summit, 15 miles east of Ashland and 23 miles west of Highway 140 junction at Lake of the Woods; elevation 5180'
Trail Length:	4.6 miles (7.4 km) round trip
Elevation Change:	Gain of 520' to Telemark Meadow
Maps:	USGS: Hyatt Reservoir (15 min.); Ashland (15 min); Emigrant Lake (7.5 min); Hyatt Reservoir (7.5 min)
	USFS/BLM: Jackson Klamath Winter Trails; BLM Medford District Maps; Rogue River National Forest

Buck Prairie Loop, the most popular in the system, has one major climb and one major downhill run; otherwise it is fairly level. It follows BLM logging roads and spurs, and also provides access to an alternate side loop to Cottonwood Glades and an overlook to the west. Part of this loop is signed for only one direction. It also has the all-important restroom at trail side.

Mile	Description
0.0	Park at Dead Indian Road Summit, where space is provided for about 15 cars. The road is marked with a large BLM sign: "Buck Prairie Road No. 38-3E-19." There are also cross-country trailhead signs and maps. Another sign warns about a local dog "Happy" who wants to follow skiers.
	Ski south along an almost level road. There are no trail markers, but you will cross a buried cattle guard about 0.5 mile along.
0.9	The wooden restroom building is on the left side. Just beyond the road branches; the lower left road drops downhill to the east (not part of the trail system); the middle road is part of the return loop; and the upper right one, marked with an orange diamond and black arrow, climbs to the top of **Telemark Meadow.**

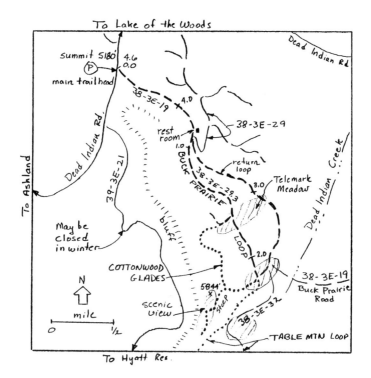

Take the upper right trail and climb uphill at about
a 10% grade.

1.7   The trail goes around a corner and enters Telemark
Meadow. There is a BLM map with plastic cover nailed
to a tree on the right. The loop trail continues
across the middle of the upper part of the meadow,
but unfortunately is only signed on the far side.
If you continue around to the right along the north
edge of the meadow, you will follow the Cottonwood
Glades Trail. If you ski downhill to the left
through the center of the meadow, you will short-cut
back to the lower part of the loop road. This route
is popular with downhill skiers. It is 0.3 mile
downhill and then 1.7 miles back to your starting
point.

Continue across the meadow and locate the orange
diamond and black arrow on the other side. The

trail enters the trees along a skid road. The only other trail marker is at the other end.

2.2   Exit onto another large meadow near its lower end. The Cottonwood Glades Trail comes around from above. Skiing uphill through the meadow will bring you to the intersection between that trail and the over-look trail. Straight ahead is the start of the Table Mountain Loop Trail marked with the standard blue diamonds. Several orange diamonds with black arrows in the meadow point to the various trails.

Turn left and ski downhill to continue on the Buck Prairie Loop.

2.3   Intersection with the Buck Prairie Road (No. 38-3E-19) and No. 38-3E-32. Continue around to the left - do not ski down to the right-center. The road that climbs uphill to the far right is the return of the Table Mountain Loop Trail. The return loop is marked with blue diamonds - seen only skiing north.

Ski slightly downhill and north.

2.9   Intersection with the bottom of Telemark Meadow at a small stream crossing. Continue downhill along the road.

3.7   Back at the outhouse and road junction. Continue over your original trail.

4.6   Parking area and trailhead on Dead Indian Road.

J2. COTTONWOOD GLADES

Trail Difficulty:	Intermediate on trail
Starting Point:	Off Buck Prairie Loop at Telemark Meadows; elevation 5600'
Trail Length:	1.1 miles (1.8 km) one way
Elevation Change:	Gain of 250' at overlook
Maps:	USGS: Hyatt Reservoir (15 min. and 7.5 min.) USFS/BLM: Jackson Klamath Winter Trails; BLM Medford District Maps; Rogue River National Forest

This trail does not go anywhere near Cottonwood Glades as it appears on the USGS maps. It does climb a ridge and offers a great view of Mt. Ashland and Bear Creek Valley to the west. From the right place you can see Mt. Shasta. It is an alternate loop off the Buck Prairie Loop Trail and signed in only one direction by orange diamonds with black arrows. The short, steep climb through heavy timber classifies the trail as intermediate.

Mile   Description

0.0   Mile 1.7 on the Buck Prairie Loop trail at
         Telemark Meadows.

         Continue slightly uphill along the north side
         of the meadow.

0.2   At the upper end of the meadow you will see a
         tree with two orange diamonds and black arrows
         pointing to the left. Start climbing uphill
         through the woods.

0.4   Top of the hill. The trail curves around to
         the right and then left.

0.5   Start downhill (it's easy to lose the trail
         at this point).

0.7   Bottom of the hill - enter a large meadow.

0.8   South side of meadow. Two orange diamonds with
         black arrows point right to the overlook trail,

and left and downhill to the continuation of
this trail. A third arrow on the right points
uphill to the overlook trail.

Ski downhill through the center of the meadow
to connect with the Buck Prairie Loop Trail at
mile 2.2.

1.1   Intersection with Buck Prairie Loop Trail. It is
           1.5 miles back to the Dead Indian Road parking
           area.

           *   *   *   *   *   *   *   *   *

           From mile 0.8 you can take a short trip to the
           westside overlook.

           Continue uphill from the south edge of the meadow
           through the trees. This is an extremely steep
           section, but well marked with orange diamonds.

           After 0.3 mile you are at the top and can ski
           along an open ridge line. A great view to the
           west and south. You can also see portions of
           the Dead Indian Road descending to Ashland.

           If you ski south along the ridge and back into
           the trees you will eventually run into the Table
           Mountain Loop Trail. This connection is not
           marked, so it was only by chance that I found
           it. It is better to return over the same trail
           to the meadow. Be careful skiing downhill
           through the trees.

           See Buck Prairie Loop Trail for map.

J3. TABLE MOUNTAIN LOOP

Trail Difficulty:	Intermediate on trail and road
Starting Point:	Mile 2.2 on the Buck Prairie Loop Trail at a large meadow; elevation 5650'
Trail Length:	5.0 miles (8.0 km) in a loop
Elevation Change:	Gain of 350' on west leg of loop and then loss of 450' to Cottonwood Glades
Maps:	USGS: Hyatt Reservoir (15 min. and 7.5 min.) USFS/BLM: Jackson Klamath Winter Trails; BLM Medford District Maps; Rogue River National Forest

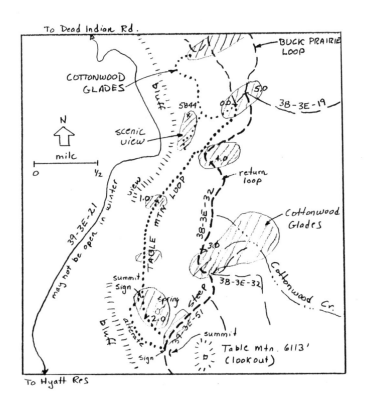

The Table Mountain Loop continues south from the Buck Prairie
Loop. The west leg of the loop follows a ridge line that
overlooks the Ashland area, and the east leg descends into and
climbs out of Cottonwood Glades. The southern end of the loop
ends within sight of Table Mountain and its lookout. A short
alternate route at the south end of the west leg of the loop is
signed only for counter clockwise travel (west leg and then east
leg) making it extremely difficult to follow in the reverse
direction unless the trail is already broken.

Mile	Description
0.0	Mile 2.2 on the Buck Prairie Loop Trail near the lower end of a large meadow. Cross the meadow and enter the trees along a trail marked with blue diamonds. This is the west leg of the loop.
	Ski slightly uphill and cross through two small clearings.
0.4	Enter along the upper edge of a large clearing. The return (east) leg of the loop follows the the road that curves around to your left about 100' away. This is a shortcut back to the parking area, 3.0 miles away.
	The trail turns right and uphill entering the trees. If you turn right about 0.1 mile ahead you can connect with the westside overlook trail by "timber bashing" to the ridge line.
1.0	Enter a large open area. In the middle a blue diamond is attached to a 4" x 4" post. Ski diagonally across the clearing. If you ski uphill to the right, you have a great view to the west.
	Continue into the woods.
1.5	Ski through another open area.
1.8	Enter the upper end of a large open area facing southeast. You may notice that snowmobiles have used this area.
	Just ahead is a sign with the cross-country skier symbol and directions: "Buck Prairie Trail" (with an arrow pointing straight ahead); "Scenic Alternate"

(with an area pointing to the right), and "Minimum snow depth 18 inches" (applying to the alternate). I believe the Buck Prairie Trail designation is wrong and should say Table Mountain Trail. At any rate the trail continues straight ahead and downhill; the alternate goes to the right.

Continue downhill across the open area and back into the trees. Climb slightly uphill.

2.3   Intersect with Road No. 39-3E-51 just below Table Mountain. This is a major snowmobile route and easily identified. To the right and uphill 0.1 mile away, the alternate route intersects this road at the summit. The return part of the loop follows this road downhill to the left.

*   *   *   *   *   *   *   *   *

The alternate loop starting at mile 1.8 turns right and then left. Major turns are marked with orange diamonds and black arrows. This trail follows the west side of the ridge providing a good view of Mt. Shasta. There are several sharp turns and one short drop between a rock outcrop.

It intersects the snowmobile road at a pass just below Table Mountain, 0.1 mile to the west of the regular trail. This point is marked with another sign with cross country skier and guidance: "5 miles to Dead Indian Road" (to the left), and 2 miles to Hyatt (to the right).

It is a short climb through the woods to the top of Table Mountain and a great 360 degree view, including one of Hyatt and Howard Prairie Reservoirs.

*   *   *   *   *   *   *   *   *

2.3   From either trail, ski to the left and downhill following the snowmobile road. The route is still marked with blue diamonds. The road descends steeply winding through several switch-backs. In fast conditions, it requires lots of control and snowplowing.

Before starting downhill, look back - note that there are no blue diamonds visible. This makes the trail hard to follow in reverse unless there is already a broken trail, something to keep in mind if you are skiing up from Campers Cover at

Hyatt Reservoir.

2.8   Bottom of the hill and intersection with Road No. 38-3E-32 . You cross Cottonwood Creek and the upper end of Cottonwood Glades. Start a long climb - you are now at the low point on the trail.

4.3   Enter a large open area where the trail is hard to follow - it curves around to the right. Just to the left, the west leg emerges from the trees at mile 0.4. You may wish to follow this route back instead of following the road; however, this later route is signed in the wrong direction.

Start downhill.

5.0   Intersection of Road No. 38-3E-32 (the one you are on) and the Buck Prarie Road No. 38-3E-19 that comes in from the right and continues on to the parking area. The Buck Prarie Loop Trail comes downhill from the left (mile 2.3). It is 2.3 miles on a gentle downhill grade to the Dead Indian Road parking area.

J4. CAMPERS COVE

Trail Difficulty:	Intermediate on road
Starting Point:	Campers Cove on the southwest end of Hyatt Reservoir, mile 9.1 on the Hyatt Prairie Road; elevation 5020'
Trail Length:	3.2 miles (5.1 km) one way
Elevation Change:	Gain of 930' to pass below Table Mt.
Maps:	USGS: Hyatt Reservoir (15 min. and 7.5 min.) USFS/BLM: Jackson Klamath Winter Trails; BLM Medford District Maps: Rogue River National Forest

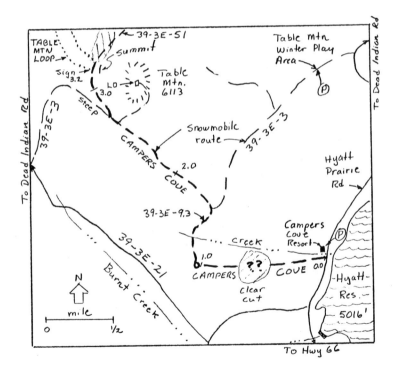

The best way to start is to ski uphill from the restaurant and store at Campers Cove. The upper end of the trail connects with the end of the Table Mountain Loop Trail below Table Mountain. The lower portion of the trail is poorly marked and difficult to follow; however, the small stream valley behind Campers Cove is easy to follow. Most ski maps show a loop trail behind Campers Cove, but I was only able to find one track and part of the signing was destroyed in a recent clearcut. Although the lower portion is on private land, there are plans to improve the signing and mark the return trail -- check with the owners of the store (address and phone are listed in the Appendix). The upper portion of the trail is used by skiers and snowmobilers.

Alternate access to the Table Mountain area is from mile 7.5 on the Hyatt Prairie Road. This turnoff is marked with a BLM sign: "Table Mtn. Winter Play Area," the Table Mtn. Road No. 39-3E-3. You can drive 0.4 mile in on this road to a winter Sno-Park. From there it is 1.8 miles uphill to the intersection with the Campers Cove Trail. This road is heavily used by snowmobilers.

Mile	Description
0.0	Park at the Campers Cove Store and Restaurant and start the trail to the left (south) of the buildings. There is a standard blue diamond marking this point. Ski uphill parallel to the fence on your right.
0.1	A split in the road; the correct route climbs to the left and the marked one continues straight ahead. If you follow the marked one to the right, it eventually enters a clear cut where the trail completely disappears. The one on the left, though not marked, eventually ties into the marked trail again. In either case, all you have to do is ski about one mile due south parallel to the stream valley and you will eventually intersect the spur road from Table Mountain. Ski up the left branch.
0.5	Enter the upper end of a clear cut. You can see the stream valley below - this is also where the other marked trail ends. Continue across this area on the road.
0.7	Enter the trees again and pick up the blue diamond signs.

1.0	Intersection with the end of the spur road from Table Mountain. Turn right and follow this road around the head of the stream valley on a level grade and then steeply uphill. It is marked with the standard blue diamonds.
1.7	Intersection with the Table Mountain Road No. 39-3E-3. Downhill and to the right will bring you to the Sno-Park area (1.8 miles).
	Turn left and ski uphill. You are now sharing the road with snowmmobilers. The trail is still marked with blue diamonds.
2.7	You are just below the summit. The road off to the right leads to the top of Table Mtn. 0.5 miles away and 200 feet higher. Keep to the left and ski over the high point.
2.8	A second road turns to the right. Do not continue straight ahead as this leads steeply downhill and eventually connects with the Burnt Creek Road No. 39-3E-21. The turn to the right is not marked, but take this road and climb uphill. You are now on Road No. 39-3E-51.
3.2	Top of the pass below Table Mountain. The ski sign on the right side of the road marks the intersection with the alternate loop of the the Table Mountain Loop Trail at mile 2.3. Just ahead and slightly downhill on the left is the intersection with the main loop. Continuing straight ahead puts you on the east leg (return leg) of the Table Mountain Loop Trail. From here it is 5.0 miles to the Dead Indian Road parking area.

K. MT. ASHLAND

Mt. Ashland, in the Siskiyou Mountains of Southern Oregon, is a granitic batholith. It is not part of the Cascades; thus it does not have landforms characteristics of volcanic eruptions and lava flows. The Siskiyou Summit, parallel to the Oregon-California border and including Mt. Ashland, has been highly sculpted by glacial and water erosion forming massive bowls on both sides of the ridge. These bowls provide an excellent place to practice telemarking.

The only winter access to the summit is from Interstate 5, about four miles north of the Oregon-California border or eleven miles south of Ashland. The Mt. Ashland ski road is plowed for nine miles west to the Mt. Ashland ski area. Most of the nordic trails start or end on this road. Only downhill ski rental is available at Mt. Ashland; however the food service is open to all. A Sno-Park permit is required to park on the road and at the ski area.

Several cross country ski trails have been marked in the vicinity of the downhill ski area, courtesy of the Rogue River National Forest. A shelter is available near Grouse Gap, just west of Mt. Ashland on the Pacific Crest Trail. It can be used on the first-come basis, maintained by the Forest Service and the Southern Oregon Chapter of the Oregon Nordic Club. Most of the ski trails are intermediate level; however a more advanced trip follows the road along the Siskiyou Summit.

The snow is generally good at Mt. Ashland since the area is around 6000'. A sudden winter storm and wind can be a major problem along the Summit Trail. These storms have been known to even close the Interstate highway over the Siskiyou summit. On a beautiful day you can see for miles: south to Mt. Shasta and north to Mt. McLoughlin and Bear Creek Valley. Check on the weather before you attempt a trip - the phone number and address of the Mt. Ashland ski area is included in the Appendix.

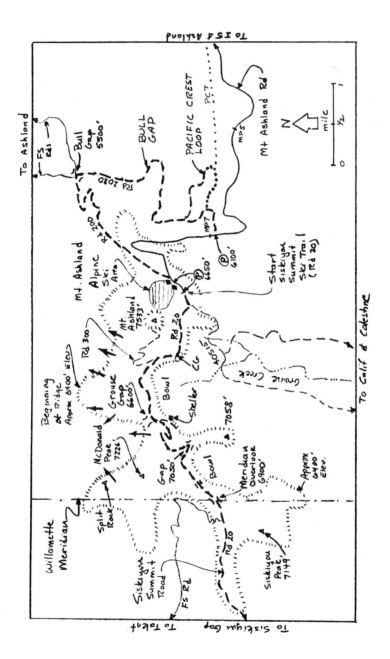

K1. SISKIYOU SUMMIT ROAD

Trail Difficulty: Intermediate on road

Starting Point: MP 9.3 on Mt. Ashland Road;
                      elevation 6650'

Trail Length: 1.9 miles (3.0 km) to Grouse Gap (elev. 6600')
                      4.0 miles (6.4 km) to Meridian Overlook
                      (elev. 6840')

Elevation change: Gain of 150 feet halfway to Grouse Gap;
                      Gain of 190 feet to Meridian Overlook

Maps: USGS: Ashland, Oregon (15 min.) and
                             Talent, Oregon (15 min.)
                      USFS: Rogue River NF and Klamath NF;
                             Map at trailhead

One of the most scenic in Southern Oregon, this trail follows Forest Service Primary Road No. 20 along the crest of the Siskiyou Mountains. The trail closely follows the watershed boundary between the Rogue River drainage and the Klamath River drainage; the boundary between the Rogue River and Klamath National Forests; and parallels the Pacific Crest Trail. Spectacular views of Mt. Shasta, Mt. McLoughlin, Pilot Rock, Ashland, Medford and the Siskiyou Mountains are seen from the saddles and adjacent ridge tops. Numerous granitic outcrops, in contrast to the Cascade volcanic rocks, dot the ridges and peaks. As an added luxury, both rest rooms and a shelter are available on the trail, and nearby Mt. Ashland alpine ski area has lodge facilities.

The trail to Grouse Gap has gradual elevation gains or losses with some sidehill traversing. Beyond Grouse Gap to Meridian Overlook the trail follows several switch backs and requires some sidehill traversing. The route also follows around several large bowls or glacial cirques that provide excellent slopes to practice telemark turns or downhill running. The main limitation of this route is weather and exposure along the ridge lines. Windy or stormy conditions can severely drift the trail making it difficult to follow. There is no alternate return route, so keep in mind that you must return over this same trail.

The trail head is at mile 9.3 on the Mt. Ashland Road, approximately 0.3 miles past the downhill ski area parking lot. Drive through this lot to the end of the plowed road, where parking is provided for skiers. A Sno-Park permit is required; obtained at the downhill ski area.

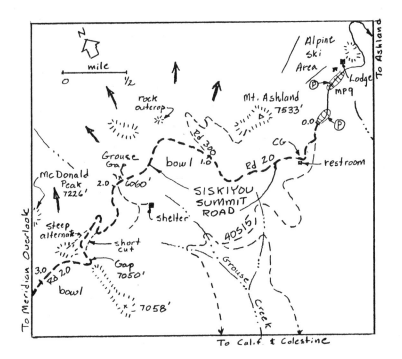

Mile   Description

0.0   Start on the other side of the barrier at the west
           end of the parking area. Snow Cat or ATV tracks may
           be apparent at this point. These are from the
           vehicle that services the radio facilities on top
           of Mt. Ashland, and catchline for errant downhill
           skiers.

0.1   Junction with Road No. 40S15 descending to the
           left. This road drops down to connecting Forest
           Service roads and eventually leads to Colestin or
           the California border. This lower road is also
           a cross-country ski trail. Dogs may accompany
           skiers on this trail. Keep to the right on Road No.
           20. The trail starts to climb slightly at this point.

0.3   Mt. Ashland camp ground with rest room facilites on
           the west side at the bend in the trail. The trail
           continues through several curves, and then comes
           into a large open bowl that provides excellent

downhill runs and areas to practice telemarking.
Grouse Gap shelter is across to the west and below
the road.

1.0   Road No. 300 bears upward to the right. This is the
       access road to Mt. Ashland, and the Snow Cat tracks
       will follow this route. The road is one mile long
       and switch backs near the top. You can use it for
       access to the ridge line and the rabbit-ear-like rock
       outcrop at the upper right. The rock outcrop is a
       good rest spot with an excellent view of Medford.
       The trail descends to Grouse Gap around the rim of
       the bowl.

       The trail at this point may be difficult to follow
       due to the adverse side slope and drifting snow.

1.9   Grouse Gap. Mt. Shasta and the surrounding valley
       are to the southeast and Medford to the northwest.
       The Pacific Crest Trail is below and Road No.
       40S30 descends to the left to Grouse Gap shelter,
       about one quarter of a mile below the gap. The
       shelter is constructed of massive stone and timber.
       It is open on two sides; however one is usually
       usually closed in with plywood (courtesy of the
       Oregon Nordic Ski Club). It has a stone fireplace,
       picnic table, and room for at least 15 to sleep
       on the ground. The open side faces Mt. Shasta
       and Pilot Rock.

       From the gap, the trail climbs uphill through the
       trees. The starting point may be a little difficult
       to see, however once you enter the trees about 100
       yards from the gap, the trail is easy to follow. It
       climbs upwards through several switch backs
       just below the ridge line. On the return trip, you
       can take the short cut easily seen from the gap at
       elevation 7050' down to the first switch back. Near
       the summit, a second trail branches off to the right,
       climbing steeply to the ridge. The road may be heavily
       drifted, making the steeper route preferable.
       Mt. Ashland with its radio tower is to the east.

2.6   Gap at elevation 7050'. At this point you leave
       the Grouse Creek bowl and enter a second bowl.
       A gap can be seen on the far side to the southwest
       McDonald Peak (elevation 7226') can be seen after
       you get around the corner to the north. McDonald
       Peak can be easily climbed by following the ridge.
       The trail is nearly level around the rim of the
       bowl. This bowl also offers excellent opportunities
       for telemarking.

3.5   Cross a cattle guard and into a gap. Switch to the
       north-facing slope and head slightly downhill.

3.8   Cross the Willammette Meridian. This meridian which
       extends south from Portland, is used by surveyors
       to describe public land subdivisions. It is the
       dividing line betwen Township 1 East (T1E) and
       Township 1 West (T1W) as seen on USGS topographic
       maps. The common corner to sections 19, 30 and 25
       is on the ridge-top to the south adjacent to the
       Pacific Crest Trail.

4.0   Meridian Overlook, named for the Willamette Meridian
       passing just east of this point. You can see the
       rest of the Siskiyou Summit along with the Applegate
       Valley to the northwest.

       Weather and snow drifting permitting, you can
       continue along USFS Road No. 20 all the way to
       Dutchman's Peak and beyond, or descend into the
       Applegate River drainage. The trail drops about
       1000 feet in the next three miles to Siskiyou Gap.
       The approximate distances from this point and
       and elevation of the proceeding landmarks are:

       Siskiyou Gap; 3 miles (5 km); elevation 5879'
       Wrangle Gap; 6 miles (10 km); elevation 6496'
       Jackson Gap; 9 miles (15 km); elevation 7061'
       Dutchmans Peak; 10.5 miles(17 km); elevation 7418'

K2. BULL GAP

Trail Difficulty:	Beginning to Bull Gap on road; Intermediate on loop to Mt. Ashland Lodge on road
Starting Point:	Sno-Park at mile 7.0 on Mt. Ashland Road; elevation 6120'
Trail Length:	3.3 miles (5.3 km) to Bull Gap; 5.8 miles (9.3 km) to Mt. Ashland Ski Area Lodge
Elevation Change:	Loss of 620 feet to Bull Gap; then gain of 1100 feet to Mt. Ashland Lodge
Maps:	USGS: Ashland (15 min.) and (7.5 min.) USFS: Rogue River National Forest

The easy skiing along this trail provides a variety of shelter in the trees and views over large clear-cut areas. It averages 3.5% downhill to Bull Gap, unfortunately requiring an uphill return trip. The return can be either over the same easy trail, or by spur road 200 to the Mt. Ashland Lodge. The latter trail, though shorter, exceeds a 10% grade in many places. My preference is to start at the Mt. Ashland ski area, travelling the steepest part downhill and then returning over the longer and more gentle uphill section in a clockwise direction. This loop trip requires a two mile connection along the Mt. Ashland Road, either by walking, skiing on the road berm, hitch-hiking, or using two cars.

There is a Sno-Park area for at least 10 cars on the right at mile 7.0 on the Mt. Ashland Highway 2.0 miles below the Mt. Ashland ski area parking lot. The trailhead is marked with a sign and a detailed trail map may be available in a plastic bag attached to the sign, courtesy of the Rogue River National Forest. Note that dogs are not allowed on this trail.

Mile	Description
0.0	Start by heading east on a fairly level trail through the woods on USFS Road 2080; marked with the standard blue diamonds.
0.4	The trail turns northwest and crosses the Pacific

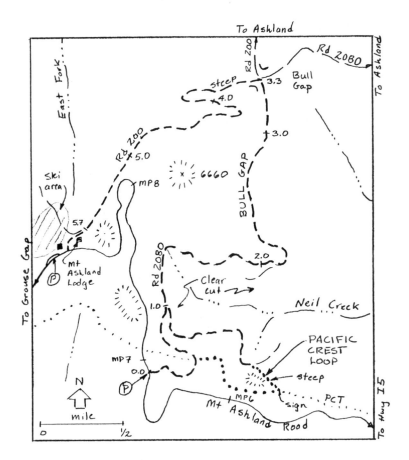

To Ashland

Rd 200

Rd 2080

To Ashland

To Ashland

steep

4.0

3.3   Bull Gap

East Fork

Rd 200 5.0

3.0

BULL GAP

Ski area

mp8

6660

5.7

Mt Ashland Lodge

P

Rd 2080

2.0

Clear cut

Neil Creek

1.0

To Grouse Gap

PACIFIC CREST LOOP

steep

mp7

0.0

N

P

mp6   sign   PcT

Mt Ashland Road

To Hwy I5

mile

0   ½

208

Crest hiking trail, marked with several "No Motor
Vehicles" signs on the left. On the right the
Pacific Crest Loop ski trail starts downhill,
marked with a "More Difficult" sign.

At this point the trail steepens.

1.0   The Pacific Crest Loop ski trail returns on a spur
        road below the trail (marked with a 2080 sign).
        A large clear-cut provides a view of the Neil Creek
        valley. Most of the next mile can be seen from
        this point, as the clear-cuts continue beyond the
        prominent point to the northeast.

1.3   Cross Neil Creek headwater and turn to the east.
        The trail is almost flat for the next half mile.
        The wind blowing through the clearcuts sculptures
        interesting snow formations and ridges along the
        road.

2.0   The trail steepens after leaving the clearcut area.
        No blue diamonds are visible beyond this point.

3.3   Bull Gap is indicated by a sign on the far side of
        this level, sheltered area. Four roads intersect
        here. Straight ahead to the north (spur 200) is
        the old Ashland Loop Road leading to Ashland,
        approximately seven miles away. The one to the
        right (east), the continuation of Road 2080, is
        the Tolman Creek Road to south Ashland. The steep
        one to the left, also Road 200, ends at the Mt.
        Ashland Lodge, 2.5 miles away.

        *   *   *   *   *   *   *   *   *   *   *   *   *

From Bull Gap you can return over the same trail or
ski to the Mt. Ashland ski area lodge. The next
description follows this latter route, an unmarked
trail following the old Ashland Loop Road, rising
1100 feet to the lodge.

Climb uphill at a 10% to 12% grade over the next mile.
The Ashland watershed is on your right.

3.8   The first switchback turns to the left.

4.2   The second switchback turns to the right as the trail
        flattens to around an 8% grade.

The next mile goes through a beautiful treelined
area. On the day I broke a trail through fresh
snow, I saw squirrel and bobcat tracks all along

this section.

5.5   The trail is just below the Mt. Ashland Road; you can hear the traffic. You can also begin to hear the downhill skiers off to the right, and you may and you may catch glimpses of the ski slopes through the trees.

5.7   Exit onto the Mt. Ashland ski slope. A sign in the middle of the trail marks the ski area boundary. The bottom of an old lift tower is just ahead, and the lodge is uphill in the distance.

5.8   Mt. Ashland Ski Area Lodge. Time for something to eat and drink and a much deserved rest....

       Note: If you are skiing this loop in a clockwise direction, start at the lodge, ski northeast below it in direct line with the old lift tower for the poma-lift. Do not ski left and downhill on Spur Road No. 210 towards the ski slope. Pass around the tower and roped-off area and head for the opening in the trees (Spur Road NO. 200), marked with the "SKI AREA BOUNDARY" sign.

K3. PACIFIC CREST LOOP

Trail Difficulty: Intermediate clockwise and
                        advanced counterclockwise on
                        a trail and logging road

Starting Point: Mile 0.4 or 1.0 on the Bull
                        Gap Trail; elevation 6000'
                        and 5920 respectively

Trail Length: 2.0 miles (3.2 km) on loop only;
                        3.4 miles (5.5 km) on loop starting
                        at the Mt. Ashland Highway Trailhead

Elevation Change: Loss of 440' from the Mt. Ashland
                        Highway Trailhead (320' on loop only)

Maps: USGS: Ashland (15 min.) and (7.5
                        min.)
                        USFS: Rogue River National Forest

This loop trail is most fun for the intermediate to advanced
skier if travelled in the counterclockwise direction. It starts
along the Pacific Crest hiking trail, then switch-backs through
the woods, and connects with a logging spur at the low point.
Like the Bull Gap Trail, you have to climb back out to the
starting point. A beginner can ski the lower portion along the
logging spur with ease. Continuing in a clockwise direction
requires a long and tiring climb through the woods.

The trail is a side loop off the Bull Gap Trail; thus the
natural starting point is at mile 7.0 on the Mt. Ashland Highway.
A Sno-Park is provided for about 10 cars. All trails are marked
with the standard blue diamonds. My trail description starts at
this point and runs in the counterclockwise direction.

Mile   Description

0.0   Start from the Mt. Ashland Highway Sno-Park and ski
                        east on a fairly level trail through the woods on
                        USFS Road 2080.

0.4   The trail turns northwest and crosses the Pacific
                        Crest hiking trail marked with several "No Motor
                        Vehicles" signs on the left. The Loop Trail is on
                        the right marked with a "More Difficult" sign.

Start downhill through the woods on the narrow Pacific Crest Trail.

0.9 The trail finally opens on an open, level area. The Mt. Ashland Highway is directly below, Mt. Shasta to the south. The trail goes into the woods again.

The trail circles counterclockwise around a small ridgeline, dropping steeply at one point.

1.2 Sign post on the Pacific Crest Trail. The continuation of the trail can be seen to the east. Leave the Pacific Crest Trail and turn north.

The trail meanders through the woods, making sharp turns that are sometimes difficult to follow. Head downhill, steeply at times, watching for the blue diamonds.

1.5 Intersection with logging spur road. This point is marked with two blue diamonds nailed to a tree, and is the low point on the trail.

Proceed uphill along the spur road. It is not marked with the blue diamonds.

1.7 Start of a clearcut. You can see the Bull Gap Trail across Neil Creek valley.

2.4 Intersection with USFS Road 2080, the Bull Gap Trail (mile 1.0). A sign with "2080" is just beyond this point. Turn left and uphill to the starting point.

3.0 Intersection with the Pacific Crest Trail, the starting point on the Loop.

3.4 Starting point on the Mt. Ashland Highway.

See Bull Gap Trail for detailed map.

APPENDIX I

HISTORY OF SOUTHERN OREGON CROSS COUNTRY SKI RACES

Crater Lake Wilderness Race

The Crater Lake Wilderness Race is the revival of a race between Fort Klamath and Crater Lake Lodge held annually from 1927 to 1938. The grueling race, originally 42 miles long, gained over 2,800 feet in elevation and challenged skiers with varying snow conditions. The race was shortened to 32 miles in 1932, five miles in 1936, and by about 1938 both the race and the accompanying winter carnival were discontinued. In 1978, the race was revived by the Alla Mage Skiers and Crater Lake National Park, and now attracts about 100 skiers annually.

The "Carnival" included snow balling, tobogganing, sleighing, short races for high school student and adults, as well as ski jumping (the record jump was 151 feet), sled dog races, bare-foot races and a homing pigeon race. There was usually an all-day dance in the community hall. The Carnival and the historic race attracted as many as 4,000 spectators.

In the early years, a sixteen mile race from the Rim to Fort Klamath was the "down mountain" or "trail breaker" race for the longer race; but later, the "down mountain" race was the more popular.

In 1927, 24 skiers entered the race. The course followed the Crater Lake Highway to the Lodge and back, with contestants required to keep within one half mile of this course. Any style, make, pattern or length of ski and harness could be used; however metal skies were barred. Manfred Jacobson, ... "a sandy haired logger"... from McCloud, California, and Waldemar Nordquist, ... "a powerful lumber piler"... from Klamath Falls, fought for first place. Jacobson had a peculiar ..."slide-slide and then skip technique like a skating stroke - his entire body swinging to the rhythm of the forward lunge." Nordquist, a former Swedish Army Captain, used arms and ski sticks more. The Evening Herald reported that the two Swedes were ..."engaged in one of the greatest battles of endurance, of wits and of the elements in the history of the Pacific Coast." Nearly every newspaper on the Pacific Coast called for bulletins. New snow made the going "tough and hard," but they arrived at the Lodge together. Jacobson had let Nordquist pass him on the way to the rim, requiring him to break trail and use precious energy. Returning downhill, Jacobson lost a ski and Nordquist a ski stick. The lead changed when they stopped to retrieve the equipment. Jacobson crossed the finish after 7 hours and 34 minutes, to win the first prize of $250. Nordquist, 21 minutes behind, won the $100 second prize. Nels Skjersaa of Bend and Everett Puckett of Klamath Falls battled for third place. Skjersaa claimed the $50 prize, and Puckett won a radio set. Harry C. Francis of Klamath Falls was fifth, winning a rifle, and Otto Hagen of Brightwood and Andy Versto of Ft. Klamath tied for sixth place.

The second race had 16 entrants: ..."stalwart athletes, most of whom bear names reminiscent of the snow-clad mountains of northern Europe." Twelve of the racers dropped out, ..."unable to keep pace with the quartet of northlanders: Manfred Jacobson, Nels Skjersaa, Waldemar Nordquist and Emil Nordeen of Bend." Jacobson won the race for a second time, in 6 hours and 13 minutes. Emil Nordeen was eight minutes behind.

In 1929, Emil Nordeen, ..."the crafty 'Old War Horse' of Bend," won the race in a record time of 5 hours 57 minutes. At 43 years, he was the oldest as well as the fastest skier. Skjersaa was second and 28 minutes behind. (Both of these men had been members of the first party to reach the top of Three-Fingered Jack in 1926.) Emil was awarded the solid silver "Klamath Cup" which stood 38 inches high and was trimmed with gold. Only three were made; the second was awarded to Charles Lindbergh when he became the first man to fly across the Atlantic Ocean, while the third was bought by Charles Curtis, U.S. Vice President under Herbert Hoover. Since the winner kept the cup only one year, a smaller 6-inch high cup called the "Shadow of Klamath" was awarded. When Emil entered the 1927 race he had to make his own race skis out of Ponderosa Pine because none were for sale.

Manfred Jacobson won in 1930, in 7 hours and 40.5 minutes. Nordeen was 34 seconds behind and Skjersaa third. The other two entrants, Nordquist and Oliver Puckett of Keno, dropped out. The racers had to battle two feet of new snow in the Park, but were forced to make a five-mile loop at the finish because there was virtually no snow at Ft. Klamath.

In 1931, there were four entrants, and only two finished. Nordeen, who almost didn't enter the race because of an injury, broke the record at 5 hours and 35 minutes and Jacobsen was second. Ivar Amoth of Bend broke a ski and Oliver Puckett dropped out after 34 miles. Nordeen had now won the Klamath Cup for the second time, thus gaining permanent possession. The Skyliner Skiing Club members of Bend carried Nordeen on their shoulders to the community hall. The newspaper reported 848 cars parked on the grounds.

In 1932, the race was shortened to 32 miles; a new ski jump was inaugurated, and buses brought spectators to the events. A record 4,000 people attended the Snow Show. This was the sixth year that Oliver Puckett had entered the long race, and with his lucky rabbit's foot, he finally won in 4 hours and 26 minutes. He was the first native born American to win the race. Pete O. Hedberg of Modoc Point was 30 minutes behind, and Rudy Lueck, a Crater Lake Ranger, was third.

Pete Hedberg, now of Klamath Falls, was the other two-time winner of the races. Also a Swede with a long history of skiing and winning races, Heberg won the 1933 race, and after poor snowfall cancelled the race in 1934, he retired the second Klamath Cup with a win in 1935. During the last race he was operating under a slight handicap; he had broken his leg several months earlier and the cast was removed only three weeks before the competition. Pete, at age 73, entered the 14-mile race in 1978 and finished with two broken poles.

Oliver Puckett almost won in 1933, but Pete Hedberg passed him in the last mile. Puckett won the second place trophy, called "The Watchman". Rudy Luech was again third. Pete's winning time was 4 hours and 30 minutes, four minutes ahead of Puckett. Rudy Luech was only a few yards behind Hedberg in the 1935 race, and Harold Paulson of Bend was third to complete the "horse race finish." Puckett led the racers to the rim, but then dropped behind on the return. Several of the racers "doped" for ice, and found soft, sticky snow, thus allowing Hedberg to win.

After the 1935 race, the Evening Herald reported ... "Skiers and officials of the Crater Lake Ski Club and Klamath Winter Sports Association are inclined strongly to the opinion that the long race is too tough, and now that Hedberg, by virtue of his two victories, has won the cup, the event might as well be dropped from the Klamath winter sports program." So, the race was shortened to five miles in 1936 and 1937. Frank Drew of Klamath Falls and Delbert Denton of Ft. Klamath were the winners these two years. Only a one mile race was held at the Crater Lake rim in 1938.

The historic races had many other heros. Myrtle Copeland of Fort Klamath entered the 1927 race with an unusual handicap; she forgot her boots and had to ski in house slippers. Needless to say she did not win, but nine years later she won the five-mile race. The Briscoe sisters of Ft. Klamath often entered and won the shorter women's race. In 1933, Ida, Vinnie and Peggie won the relay race. The Drew family of Klamath Falls also had winners in many of the shorter races. Frank and Greer often competed for first and second place in the high school and college student races. Lester Hellens of Seattle and Millard Biscoe of Wood River won the first two "down races."

In 1964, Emil Nordeen donated his Klamath Cup to the Swedish Ski Association at the Squaw Valley Olympic Games. The cup was subsequently used in team races in Sweden and finally retired.

In 1980, with the aid of Jay Bowerman, two-time U.S. Olympic Biathalon Team Member, and the Bend Bulletin newspaper, the Swedes agreed to award the cup in the 37-mile Kalvtraskloppet race in northern Sweden. The race, which draws about 1000 skiers, starts 30 miles from Nordeen's birthplace of Norsjo. The trophy will remain in a museum in Umea near the race site, and the winner will receive either a small replica or a photograph-diploma symbolic of victory.

Unpredictable snow conditions have forced the sponsoring groups to keep the modern races totally within Crater Lake National Park. Four races are usually planned for around the second weekend in February, covering distances of 10, 15, 24 and 39 kilometers (6, 9, 15 and 24 miles). Because of the terrain and wilderness conditions in the park, the courses are not machine-groomed but are set by skiers. They begin and end near Park Headquarters. Emil Nordeen, then 81, started the 1978 race. Gary Dalesky of Bend, my former OIT ski student, won the long race and many of the later races.

1978 Crater Lake Ski Race: Pete Hedberg, Emil Nordeen, the author, Gary Dalesky

Photos courtesy of Pete Hedberg, Emil Nordeen and Klamath County Museum.

John Day Nordic Memorial Ski Race

The John Day Nordic Memorial Races at Diamond Lake are sponsored by the Oregon Nordic Club and Diamond Lake Nordic Center. Two races, at 9 km and 18 km (5.6 and 11.2 miles), are on groomed tracks along the east side of the lake. The first annual race was held in late February 1987. John Day, who passed away in 1986, stimulated much of today's interest in Nordic skiing. He has even been called the "Johnny Appleseed" of cross country skiing. Day, owner of the Gold Rey Buffalo Ranch near Central Point, Oregon, was the U.S. Director for Citizen Skiing (Cross Country) for the International Ski Federation.

When John was 46, his doctors told him he would never walk erect again due to severe arthritis in his back. He decided to prove them wrong and began a rigorous hiking program. He later climbed all six major peaks in Washington State in nine days, and over 250 other major peaks. He climbed Mt. McKinley in 1960 and broke both legs and ankles in a fall during the descent. A helicopter pilot plucked him off the mountain in the first high altitude chopper rescue on record.

After partially recovering, he decided to take up cross country skiing to reduce the strain on his legs. Since there were few instructors in the U.S. at that time, he went to Norway to learn how to ski. He mastered the Norwegian techniques and later entered the grueling 60-mile Hardanger Katjulen ski race, finishing it in 17 hours. At 55, he asked to try out for the 1964 U.S. Olympic ski team, but was turned down.

He wanted to promote skiing in the U.S., a hard task since the sport had taken a back seat for 25 years. First he asked Michael Brady to translate a popular Norwegian ski training book into English and published 2,000 copies at his own expense. Then he spent the winter of 1965 travelling around the country, carrying his book, skies and waxes, promoting the sport. He invited the Italian National Team coach and his two top skiers to Oregon for a training clinic. They ended their visit by skiing the Crater Lake Rim in a record six and one-half hours.

In 1966, he founded the Oregon Nordic Club, and received the club's first award. He also entered many ski races, winning the gold medal at the 1983 World Masters Championships at Telemark, Wisconsin in the 3 x 10 K relay. He has also skied in the races at Crater Lake National Park.

I first met John Day at an Oregon Nordic Club race at Crater Lake National Park, where he presented the trophies for the 1968 race. I was last in my class, handicapped by a rotten wax job, but won a third-place trophy. Once I raced with him when he had two broken ribs - he won his age class that day.

REFERENCES: Herald and News, Klamath Falls, Oregon - articles:
Jan. 26, 1975 (Bruce Meadows), Feb. 9, 1978 (Lee
Juillerat), Feb. 10, 1978, Feb. 22, 1978, Mar.
23, 1978 (Lee Juillerat), and Feb. 6, 1987
(Cathrine Harris).

Evening Herald, Klamath Falls, Oregon - various
articles, 1927 through 1938.

The Bulletin, Bend, Oregon - article: Jan. 26,
1987

1986 Ski X-C, "The Legendary John Day" By Bob
Woodward, CBS Magazines, NY, 1985

Crater Lake 1977: **Dave Lund, John Day, and the** author

APPENDIX II

RESORT ADDRESSES

LEMOLO LAKE RESORT
HC 60, Box 79 B
Idelyld Park, OR 97447
Mobile phone: JS2-7060
(On Glide Channel)

DIAMOND LAKE RESORT
Diamond Lake, OR 97731
503-793-3333
(Nordic Center has the
same address and phone)

CRATER LAKE LODGE CO.
PO Box 97
Crater Lake, OR 97604
503-594-2511
(Same address and phone
for ski rentals)

UNION CREEK RESORT
Prospect, OR   97536
503-560-3565

ROCKY POINT RESORT
HC 34, Box 92
Klamath Falls, OR 97601
503-356-2287

LAKE OF THE WOODS RESORT
Box 950 Harriman Rt.
Klamath Falls, OR 97601
503-949-8300

FISH LAKE RESORT
PO Box 40
Medford, OR   97501
503-949-8500

WARNER CANYON SKI AREA
%Fremont Highlanders Ski Club
PO Box 1204
Lakeview, OR.   97630
503-947-2932

CAMPERS COVE
PO Box 222
Ashland, OR 97520
503-482-1201

SKI ASHLAND, INC.
PO Box 220
Ashland, OR   97520
503-482-2897 (office)
503-482-2754 (snow phone)

SKI CLUB ADDRESSES

ALLA MAGE SKIERS
PO Box 7705
Klamath Falls, OR   97601

FREMONT HIGHLANDERS SKI CLUB
PO Box 1204
Lakeview, OR   97630

GRANTS PASS NORDIC CLUB
%Taylor Cain
211 SW Oak St.
Grants Pass, OR   97526

SOUTHERN OREGON CHAPTER
OREGON NORDIC CLUB
%Steve Parsons
Phoenix, OR   97535

FEDERAL AGENCY ADDRESSES

UMPQUA NATIONAL FOREST

Forest Supervisor
PO Box 1008
Roseburg, OR 97470
503-672-6601

Diamond Lake Ranger District
HC 60, Box 101
Idleyld Park, OR 97447
503-498-2531

ROGUE RIVER NATIONAL FOREST

Forest Supervisor
PO Box 520
Medford, OR 97501
503-776-3600

Ashland Ranger District
645 Washington St.
Ashland, OR 97520
503-482-3333

Butte Falls Ranger District
PO Box 227
Butte Falls, OR 97522
503-865-3581

Prospect Ranger District
Prospect, OR 97536
503-560-3623

WINEMA NATIONAL FOREST

Forest Supervisor
2819 Dahlia St.
Klamath Falls, OR 97601
503-883-6714

Chemult Ranger District
PO Box 150
Chemult, OR 97731
503-365-2229

Klamath Ranger District
1936 California Ave.
Klamath Falls, OR 97601
503-883-6824

FREMONT NATIONAL FOREST

Forest Supervisor
PO Box 551
Lakeview, OR 97630
503-947-2151

Bly Ranger District
PO Box 25
Bly, OR 97622
503-353-2427

Lakeview Ranger District
Highway 395 N
Lakeview, OR 97630
503-947-3334

BUREAU OF LAND MANAGEMENT

Medford District
3040 Biddle Road
Medford, OR 97501
503-776-4174

CRATER LAKE NATIONAL PARK

Superintendent
Crater Lake National Park
PO Box 7
Crater Lake, OR 9760

Weather information
and road conditions
503-594-2211

GEOLOGICAL SURVEY TOPOGRAPHIC MAPS

U.S. Department of Interior
Geological Survey
Branch of Distribution
Box 25286
Denver Federal Center
Denver, CO 80225